FIJI

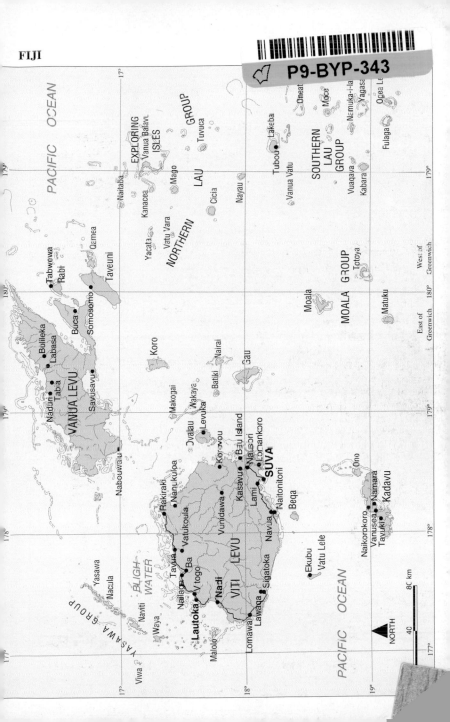

Fiji

Fay Smith

Little Hills Press

© Little Hills Press, 1999
Second Edition, April 1999
Photographs by Fiji Tourist Bureau
Cover by Artitude
Maps by MAPgraphics and Mark & Angela Butler
Printed in Singapore

ISBN 186315 129 X

Little Hills Press Pty Ltd
Regent House
37-43 Alexander Street
Crows Nest NSW 2065
Australia

Front Cover: Fijian entertainer dressed for a traditional Fijian Meke Night
Back Cover: Water fun on Castaway island.

CONTENTS

Introduction

The Fijian archipelago includes more than 300 islands scattered across some 230,000 sq km of the south-west Pacific Ocean, crossing the 180th meridian between 15 and 19 degrees south of the Equator. Over 100 of the islands are inhabited, the remainder are 'desert' islands, having no source of fresh water.

The two largest islands of the group, Viti Levu and Vanua Levu, comprise 85% of the total land mass. The third in size is Taveuni, which has some of the most beautiful tropical forests in Fiji, and a stone marking the 180th meridian and the original course of the International Dateline.

The rest of the islands are divided into four smaller groups - the *Mamanucas*, off the west coast of Viti Levu; the *Yasawa* chain, to the north-west; the *Lomaiviti* islands, in the Koro Sea between Vanua Levu and Viti Levu; and the *Lau* group, to the east and south of the two main islands. Some of the Fijian islands are surrounded wholly or in part by coral reefs that form natural harbours and deep lagoons. The larger islands are primarily volcanic in origin with high rugged peaks that typify this type of formation. The smaller islands are mainly coral or limestone. The chief products are: coconuts, forest products, sugar, beer, cement and cigarettes.

The capital of the republic is Suva. The international airport is at Nadi, and is 1710km north-east of Sydney; 1164km north of Auckland; 2756km south-west of Honolulu; and 3851km south-east of Tokyo.

HISTORY

Archaeologists have found pottery in Fiji that suggests the islands may have been settled by Polynesians around 1500BC. Other discoveries suggest that the Melanesian people joined them about 500BC. Whatever their origins, the people engaged in continual warfare, and were extremely barbaric and cruel. They were cannibals, but even more. If they captured a particularly hated person they would chop off an ear, nose or hand, maybe cook it in front of him, and then offer him first bite. Small wonder Fiji was once known as the 'Cannibal Isles'.

European Discovery

The Dutch explorer Abel Tasman sighted the eastern islands in 1643, but did not land. Captain Cook, the famous British navigator and explorer, visited Vatoa (Turtle Island), one of the southern islands, in 1774. The first European to see the main islands was Captain William Bligh. In 1789 he passed through them after the *Bounty* mutiny on his open-boat voyage to Timor, and made the first chart of the area. He and his crew were chased by canoe-loads of cannibals in a stretch of water now known as Bligh Sea.

Early explorers all stressed the danger of Fiji. Warring tribes, cannibals, and the reefs surrounding the islands made sailors wary of exploration.

In January 1800, came Fiji's first real contact with the outside world when the American schooner *Argo* was wrecked on Bukatatanoa reef in the Lau group. Only one crewman was killed during the foundering, but only one sailor survived contact with the Fijians. The man's name was Oliver Slater, and he lived for a time in a village on Bua Bay at the western tip of Vanua Levu. In a way the crew of the *Argo* got their revenge on the Fijians, as the brief contact between the two peoples exposed the Fijians to a new germ. Lacking immunity due to their natural quarantine by the Pacific, the sickness, which was probably Asian Cholera, soon reached epidemic proportions. The natives called it *na lila balavu,* which can translate as 'the long skinny' or as 'the withering sickness'. The epidemic lasted for months, and in many villages there were not enough people fit enough to bury the dead.

In 1803, after the plague had ran its course, a ship called *El Plumier* anchored in Bua Bay and rescued Oliver Slater, who finally managed to work his way to Sydney. Here he told of the large groves of sandalwood that grew in the Bua Bay area, and within days ships were being provisioned to make the journey to Fiji. Slater sailed aboard one of the first of these, and used his knowledge of the language to facilitate the rape of the forests in return for worthless trinkets.

Fiji's years of isolation were over with the influx of foreign ships after sandalwood, and later, others came for *bche de-mer*, a sea slug considered to be a delicacy in Asia. Whalers also began calling into the islands for provisions. Along with all these visitors came firearms and alcohol, which would bode no good in the future for the inexperienced Fijians.

And the fate of Oliver Slater? He lived for many years on the islands, but for some unknown reason was clubbed to death as he slept in a village on Makogai island.

Missionaries

The first Christian missionaries, two Protestant Tahitians, arrived at Lakeba in 1830, followed by two Wesleyan Europeans in 1835. The missionaries made little headway until they settled near the small island of Bau off the south-west corner of Viti Levu in 1839. Bau was the headquarters of a chief named Cakobau who had much influence over the coastal villages of Viti Levu and many of the islands to the east. By 1850 he was commonly known as *Tui Viti*, King of Fiji. Later some of his people revolted against him, and he thought that if he embraced Christianity, peace would be restored. He was right. Much of the fighting ceased and cannibalism was abandoned.

European Settlers

Cakobau faced debts arising from claims by a former American Consul, John B. Williams. When W.T. Pritchard arrived as the first British Consul in 1858, Cakobau offered to cede his islands to Britain if they would pay his debts. Pritchard went to London to put the case before the government who sent two investigators to examine the country's potential.

Rumours that Fiji would become a British colony brought many Europeans to settle. These pioneers made numerous attempts to establish a stable government under Cakobau's authority, but they failed. On October 10 1874, Britain accepted a second offer of cession and Fiji became a Crown Colony with the capital at Levuka. It was moved to Suva in 1882.

When the first British Governor, Sir Arthur Gordon, arrived, the economy was stagnant. He thought growing sugar was the best way to revive the economy, but feared that large scale employment of Fijians as labourers would disrupt their traditional way of life, so he authorised the importation of Indians to work the sugar plantations. The first Indians arrived in 1879 under an indenture system that lasted until 1916. Many stayed on after their contracts expired, and by 1946 the Indians outnumbered the Fijians.

Fiji became independent on October 10 1970. Ratu Sir Kamisese Mara, a Fijian chief, led a multi-racial Fijian dominated government until 1987. In the fifth election since independence he was defeated by Timoci Bavadra, the Fijian leader of an Indian dominated coalition. In May 1987, the army led by Colonel Sitiveni Rambuka overthrew the government, and a second coup in September 1987 consolidated Rambuka's hold. Fiji then became a republic, and the government promised to ensure democracy, but many of the Indian population left the country. The 1992 elections resulted in a coalition victory with Rambuka as Prime Minister. The new constitution prevents the army from taking control.

CLIMATE

With a warm and pleasant climate throughout the year, Fiji is an ideal holiday destination. It has a subtropical climate without extremes of hot and cold. The best time to visit is April to October when it is mild and dry with temperatures ranging from 23˚C to 30˚C. The warm wet season is November to March with temperatures from 20C to 36C, and the possibility of cyclones.

POPULATION

The total population is 781,000, made up of 50% Fijians, 46% Indians and the remainder are Chinese, Rotuman (from the small island of Rotuma, north of Fiji) and European.

LANGUAGE

English is the official language, but Fijian is widely spoken, so most people are bilingual. The first day you are in Fiji you will become accustomed to greeting, and being greeted by, everyone with the traditional 'bula', which means 'good health', but here are a few other words to add to your vocabulary.

Firstly, there are a few pronunciation rules -

'b' - 'mb' as in bamboo
'c' - 'th' as in this
'd' - 'nd' as in candy
'g' - 'ng' as in singer
'q' - 'ngg' as in finger

Good morning	Ni sayadra *(nee sah yahn-dra)*
Please	Yalo vinaka *(yahlo vee-naka)*
Thank you/good	Vinaka *(vee-nahka)*
Yes	Io *(ee-oh)*
No	Sega *(seng-ah)*
Eat	Kana *(kah-na)*
Lady/woman	Marama *(marama)*
Man	Turaga *(too-rahng-ah)*
Small	Lailai *(lie-lie)*
Large	Levu *(lay-voo)*
A little	Vakalailai *(vaka lei-lei)*
A lot	Vakalevu *(vaka lay-voo)*
Quickly	Vakatotolo *(vaka-teo-toe-low)*
Slowly	Vaka malua *(vaka ma-loo-ah)*
House	Vale *(val-lay)*
Toilet	Valelailai *(Val-lay-lie-lie)*
Come	Lako mai *(lah-ko-my)*.

RELIGION

Christianity, Hinduism and Islam are practised. About 50% are Christians, 10% Muslims. Following is a list of Christian churches in Suva, with times of services. If you are not staying in Suva, your hotel desk will have details of churches in their area.

Anglican Holy Trinity Cathedral,
18 MacArthur Street - 7.30am, 10am.
Assemblies of God,
11 Anand Street (off Robertson Road) - 10.30am.
Methodist Church,
Wesley Circuit Mission, Butt Street - 8am, 10.45am, 5pm
Presbyterian St Andrews Church,
cnr Gordon & Goodenough Streets - 10am
Roman Catholic Sacred Heart Cathedral,
Pratt Street - 7am, 8.30am, 10am, 7pm
Salvation Army,
Grantham Road - 11am, cnr Suva & Spring Streets - 6pm
Seventh Day Adventist,
Princes Road, Tamavua - (Saturday) 9am.

FESTIVALS

Bula Festival -
in July. The festival which is held in Nadi every year lasts a week.

Hibiscus Festival -
Fiji's carnival of the year. Held in Suva during August to coincide with school holidays. Lasts one week.

Sugar Festival -
in September. The sugar city of Lautoka comes alive with the annual festival.

Diwali Festival -
Held in the first half of the Hindu month of Kartika (October\November) this is the Festival of Lights, commonly called Diwali. Hindu homes are elaborately decorated with lights.

Traditions - Legends
Firewalking
The unsolved mystery of how Fijians from the island of Beqa can walk on white hot rocks is seen in the spectacular ritual of firewalking. The firewalkers attribute their power to the God Veli. The Hindu ritual of firewalking is also carried out in Fiji.

The Tabua
Originally the Tabuas were highly polished pieces of wood from the bua tree. When the whalers first visited Fiji, they brought whales teeth to use for trading. The Fijians were struck by the similarity of the whale's teeth to their wooden Bua-ta. The whalers named them Tabua, from the word 'tabu' meaning sacred.

The Tabua is highly valued in tradition. To be presented with one is a great honour. It is not permitted to take a Tabua out of Fiji without an export licence from the Ministry of Fijian Affairs.

Calling of the Turtles

On the island of Kadavu, the maidens of the village of Namuana sing a strange chant that brings the large sea turtles to the surface to listen to the music. This unusual phenomenon does indeed take place and is based on an ancient legend.

Red Prawns

Legend has it that these red prawns were once a gift to the daughter of the chief of Vatulele. The daughter was so disgusted with the gift that she had the prawns thrown from the cliffs. Today, these sacred prawns can be found in pools under the cliffs.

Yaqona (Kava)

The yaqona (pronounced yangona) ceremony is very important in Fijian life, but the drink is also a social beverage, and it is not unusual to see groups indulging in their favourite 'poison'.

Yaqona is made from the root of a pepper tree, *Piper methysticum,* which is pounded into a soft pulpy mass. In olden days this was achieved by the young girls of a village who chewed the pieces of root, but nowadays a mortar and pestle, or even a machine, are used. Water is added, then the mixture is strained through cloth. The ancient way was to strain it through a bundle of shredded bark from the vau tree.

Yaqona looks (and tastes) like dirty dish water, but sampling it is one of those things you just have to do, and drinking it socially is not going to interfere with tradition - it does tend to creep up on you though, so watch out. When your lips become numb, you have had enough.

The yaqona ceremony has hard and fast rules. The guest of honour sits cross-legged in front of the tanoa, a wooden bowl carved from a single piece of vesi hardwood. Protruding from the tanoa is a thick rope made from coconut fibre and decorated with cowrie shells, which is called Tui-ni-Buli. This is pointed towards the guest of honour, and woe betide anyone who crosses this line during the ceremony.

The emcee orders water to be added to the root, and when he is satisfied with the quantity, the yaqona is strained and the cup-bearer presents the guest with the first bowl. This has to be drained in a single draught, then there is a cry of *maca,* which means 'it is drained', and much clapping of hands. The next person to drink is the emcee, then it is in order of rank.

Visitors can attend yaqona ceremonies, which are always held at night, but for a social drink call into the Fiji Visitor's Bureau and along with the drink you will get a certificate of membership to the *Fellowship of Fiji Kava Drinkers.*

Public Holidays

January 1	New Year's Day
March 12	National Youth Day
April 3/5	Good Friday/Easter Monday
May 31	Ratu Sukuna Day
June 12	Queen's Birthday
July 26	Constitution Day
July 28	Mohammed's Birthday
October 11	Fiji Day
November 8	Diwali
December 25	Christmas Day
December 26	Boxing day.

ENTRY REGULATIONS

A passport valid for at least three months beyond the length of stay is required and a ticket for onward travel. Visas for 30 days are issued to Commonwealth visitors on arrival. Other nationals should check with their travel agent before leaving their home country. Vaccinations are not required unless entering from a designated infected area.

Duty Free Allowance

Travellers over the age of 18 are allowed to import the following free of duty: 500 cigarettes or 500gm of cigars or 500gm of tobacco or a combination of all three provided the total does not exceed 500gm. 2 litres of liquor or 4 litres of wine or 4 litres of beer.

Up to F$400 (US$267) per passenger of any duty assessed goods.

Exit Formalities

There is a departure tax of F$20 (about US$15) levied on all travellers over 12 years of age. It is payable in local currency.

Embassies

Australia:
37 Princess Road, Tamavua, ph 382 211, fax 382 065.

Canada:
Honorary Consul, PO Box 1932, Nadi,
ph 750 400, fax 750 666.

New Zealand:
Reserve Bank Building, Pratt Street, Suva,
ph 311 422, fax 300 842.

United States of America:
31 Loftus Street, Suva,
ph 314 466, fax 300 081.

United Kingdom:
47 Gladstone Road, Suva,
ph 311 033, fax 301 406.

MONEY

The basic unit of currency is the Fijian dollar.
Notes come in denominations of $2, $5, $10, $20, $50, and coins
are 1c, 2c, 5c, 10c, 20c, 50c, $1.

Approximate rates of exchange are:

A$	F$1.22
Can$	F$1.16
NZ$	F$1.04
UK£	F$3.35
US$	F$2.00

As the rate of exchange varies, check before changing money. Most major credit cards are accepted by hotels. Please note that most hotels require an imprint of a credit card on check-in or a substantial cash deposit to cover incidentals over and above your accommodation charges.

There is a 10% goods and service tax - VAT.

Banks

Australia & New Zealand Banking Group (ANZ), Westpac, National Bank of Fiji, Bank of Baroda, Habib Bank and the Bank of Hawaii are all represented in Suva and Nadi. There are also agencies throughout Fiji.

COMMUNICATIONS

International Direct Dialling is available and the country code is 679. No area code is required, simply dial the Fiji number. Outer islands in the Fiji group not on direct dialling, are serviced by a radio telephone system.

Fax and telex services are available through FINTEL (Fiji's telecommunications operator), ph 312 933, fax 305 606. Facilities are available in most major hotels. Public telephones take 10c coins for local calls, which cost 20c, and can be found at all post offices. Phone cards are available.

There are two English language daily newspapers, the *Fiji Times* and *Fiji Sun*. Fijian and Hindi language newspapers are published weekly. TV programs are from Australia and New Zealand. There is a local radio station.

MISCELANEOUS

Time
Local time is GMT + 12.

Business Hours
Banks:
Mon-Thurs 9.30am-3pm - Fri 9.30am-4pm.
There is a 24hr service at Nadi Airport.

Post Offices:
Mon-Fri 8am-4.30pm, closed for lunch 1-2pm. Sat 8.am-11.00am.

Government Offices:
Mon-Thurs 8am-4.30pm - Fri 8am-4.00pm. Closed for lunch 1-2pm.

Commercial outlets,
including vegetable and handicraft markets are open five days a week and half day Saturday. There is little open on Sundays and Public Holidays.

Electricity
Supply is 240V AC 50 HZ, and three-pin plugs, as used in Australia and New Zealand, are found in hotels. If your appliances are 110V you will need a converter.

Credit Cards
Major cards are accepted by hotels and businesses. American Express Suva, can replace lost credit cards and travellers cheques. Diners Club, Visa, JCB and Mastercard are represented in Suva.

Tipping
Tipping is not expected nor encouraged. All hotels have a Staff Christmas Fund and contributions may be made to this fund for exceptional service.

Health

Fiji is free from most tropical diseases including malaria. No vaccinations are required unless coming from an infected area. Hospitals are located in Suva, Sigatoka, Lautoka, Savusavu and Nadi. Most towns have a government clinic staffed by a District Nurse. There is a reasonable charge for patients who are not citizens of Fiji. Private medical services are also available.

Drinking water is safe in all cities, resorts and urban areas but it is advisable to buy bottled water in outlying districts.

Insurance

It is advisable to take out full travel insurance, especially medical.

Emergency Telephone Numbers

Fire, Police, Ambulance - 000.

Weights and Measures

Fiji uses the metric system.

Etiquette

Clothing should be suitable for a warm climate but modest. Always carry a sulu to cover bathing togs, shorts and halter tops.

Do not wear a hat or cap in a village as it is considered to be an insult to the chief. Do not wear shoes in people's houses.

It is considered an insult to touch someone's head.

When visiting a village it is customary to present a gift of Yaqona. Half-a-kilo costs about A$10 (US$6).

Observing the Fijian customs will make you a welcome guest in their homes, and will enhance your holiday.

Photography

Most locals do not object to having their photo taken. The main problem is that they want to pose so candid shots are hard to take. The latest photographic equipment is available in Fiji, as is same day processing in major centres.

Travel Information

HOW TO GET THERE

By Air

Air Pacific has regular flights from Sydney, Brisbane, Melbourne, Christchurch, Honiara, Tonga, Apia, Tokyo and Port Vila to Nadi and from Tonga and Apia to Suva.

Qantas flights arrive at Nadi from Australia, Honolulu, San Francisco, Los Angeles and Vancouver. Air New Zealand, Air Vanuatu, Air Nauru, Air Caledonie, Air India, Canadian Airlines, Polynesian Airlines, Singapore Airlines and Solomon Airlines have regular flights to Fiji.

Domestic Airlines

Air Fiji Ltd, Sunflower Airlines and Vanya Air have regular domestic services, and Turtle Airways have sea-plane flights to the outer islands. Flights from Nadi to Suva take about 40 minutes.

Airport Facilities

Nadi International Airport is open 24 hours a day, and the Fiji Visitors Bureau at the Arrivals Concourse is also staffed 24 hours a day.

The airport has the usual services - duty free shopping, restaurants, bar, bank/currency exchange, left luggage office, rental car agencies, post office.

Airline Telephone Numbers

	Suva	Nadi	Fax
Air Caledonie	302 133	722 145	fax 720 236
Air India	315 055	722 521	fax 300 771
Air New Zealand	313 100	722 955	fax 302 294
Air Pacific	304 388	720 888	fax 721 990
Air Vanuatu	315 055	722 521	fax 300 771
Canadian	311 844	722 400	fax 305 800
Polynesian	315 05,		fax 300 771
Qantas	313 888	722 880	fax 300 434
Singapore	302 333	722 325	
Solomon	315 889	722 831	fax 720 346
Air Fiji	313 666	722 521	fax 400 479
Sunflower	315 755	723 016	fax 723 611
Turtle	722 389		fax 722 988
Vanua Air Charter	313510		fax 386 460

Transport from the Airport

Most hotels and motels have courtesy bus transfer from the airport, or there is a public bus service that operates to major towns daily 6am-9.30pm.

Airport taxis operate 24 hours a day, and their meters apply for travel up to 15km. Fares for longer distances must be negotiated, before you get into the cab. From the airport to hotels in the Nadi area the fare ranges from F$2 to F$6.

Distances from the airport are:

Nadi Town	9km
Lautoka City	24km
Sigatoka Town	70km
Korolevu	101km
Pacific Harbour	148km
Suva City	197km

By Sea

Many cruise ships call at Suva and Lautoka.

TOURIST INFORMATION

Fiji Visitors Bureau has an office in:

Thomson Street, Suva, **ph 302 433, fax 300 970,**

and one at Nadi Airport, **ph 722 433, fax 720 141.**

Up to date tourist information is distributed free through hotels.

ACCOMMODATION

There is no shortage of accommodation in Fiji, the only problem is making up your mind what type of accommodation to choose - international standard resort, large town hotel, island resort or bure (Fijian native house). If you are opting for one of the large 'up-market resorts, it is a good idea to pack some smart/casual gear, as some of them have dress regulations for their top restaurants, and for managers cocktail parties, etc.

Following are some examples of what's available, with prices for a night's stay, which should be used as a guide only.

Nadi
Moderate Class

Tanoa Apartments, PO Box 9203, Nadi Airport,

ph 723 685, fax 721 193.

3 minutes from Nadi Airport and 10 minutes from Nadi town. Set on a hillside with view of Nadi Bay, but not near beach. 23 self-contained serviced apartments 1-2 bedrooms. Continental breakfast included, use of all facilities at Tanoa International (free shuttle). Ideal base for larger families.

Price A$140-190 (US$90-124).

Tanoa International, PO Box 9203, Nadi Airport,

ph 720 277, fax 720 191.

3 minutes from Nadi Airport and 10 minutes from Nadi town. Not near beach. 114 rooms with 1 double bed, 1 sofa bed. Daytime

child-minding, babysitting, children's playground and pool. Refurbished and suitable for long or short stays.
Price twin share A$63-70 (US$41-45), single A$125-140 (US$81-91).

Fiji Mocambo, PO Box 9195, Nadi Airport,
ph 722 000, fax 720 324.
3 minutes from Nadi Airport, 10 minutes from Nadi town. Nice view, but not near beach. 124 rooms with one queen size bed. Babysitting, child menus, high chairs, cots. 9-hole golf course, restaurants, bars, lively night-time atmosphere. Price twin share **A$62-123 (US$40-80), single A$125-246 (US$81-160), child 2-15 free.**

Tokatoka Resort, PO Box 9305, Nadi Airport,
ph 720 22, fax 720 400.
2 minutes from Nadi Airport and 10 minutes from Nadi town. Not near beach. 20 Villa apartments, 20 Villa studios, plus apartment suites and apartment studios. Playground/pool complex. All rooms have cooking facilities, supermarket on-site. Good value for families.
Price twin share A$51-62 (US$33-40), single A$102-123 (US$66-80), child 2-15 free.

Standard Class
Club Fiji, Wailoaloa Beach, Nadi Bay,
ph 702 189, fax 702 324.
15 minute drive from Nadi Airport, 10 minutes from Nadi town. 254 timber thatched bures all facing beach, with one queen bed and one single divan. Family bures, baby sitting, highchairs and cots. Windsurfing, paddle boards, waterskiing, scuba diving, horseriding, sailing, excursions. Well run resort with good food. Suit budget-conscious looking for beach location.
Price twin share A$35-63 (US$23-41), single A$70-126 (US$45-82).

Skylodge, PO Box 9222, Nadi Airport,
ph 722 200, fax 720 212.
5 minutes from Nadi Airport, and midway between airport and
Nadi town. Not near beach. 49 rooms with one double and one
single bed. Baby sitting, cots, playground, kids under 13 eat free.
Set in 4.45 hectares of garden. Well suited for those on a budget
and families. Ideal base for day tours and excursions.
**Price twin share A\$45-55 (US\$30-36), single A\$70-126
(US\$45-82), child 2-15 free.**

Raffles Gateway, PO Box 9891, Nadi Airport,
ph 722 444, fax 720 620.
Opposite Nadi Airport, 10 minutes from Nadi town. 22 standard
rooms and 5 suites with one queen and one single bed. Baby
sitting, video hire, highchairs, cots, playground. Ideal for early
starts or late arrivals. Bar, restaurant, swimming pool.
**Price twin share A\$44-56 (US\$28-36), single A\$88-112
(US\$57-73).**

Budget
New Westgate, PO Box 10097, Nadi Airport,
ph 720 044, fax 720 071.
10 minutes from Nadi Airport, 5 minutes from Nadi town. Not
near beach. 35 rooms with double and single bed. Baby sitting,
cots, high chairs, children's menus, video. 'Jessica's' nightclub is
one of Nadi's hottest night spots. Recommended for overnight or
short stays.
**Price twin share A\$60 (US\$39), single A\$72 (US\$47), child
2-15 free.**

Coconut Inn, 37 Vunavau Road,
ph 701 011, fax 701 169.
In centre of Nadi town. 22 rooms air-conditioning, fans, tea and
coffee making facilities. Restaurant, bar. Tours and cruises available.
Price A\$25-45 (US\$16-29).

Horizon Beach Resort, PO Box 1401, Nadi,
ph 722 832, fax 720 662.
A few minutes from Nadi Beach, 4 minutes from 18-hole golf course, complimentary green fee. Close to Nadi airport and town. Activities include volleyball, diving, fishing, horseback riding, tours and cruises. Restaurant, bar, TV lounge, courtesy transport. Single and double air-conditioned rooms
Price A$30-40 (US$20-26).

Melanesian Hotel, PO Box 10410, Nadi,
ph 722 438, fax 720 425.
Five minutes from airport, beach and golf course. All rooms with private facilities, tea and coffee making, phones and baby-sitting. Pool, courtesy airport transfers, handy to tours and cruises.
Price A$28-40 (US$18-26), dormitory A$8 (US$5).

Sandalwood Inn, PO Box 9454, Nadi Airport,
ph 722 044, fax 720 103.
25 rooms and 12 lodge rooms with kitchenette. Courtesy airport transfers. Air-conditioned or fans with private facilities, tea/coffee making, fridge. ISD dialling from lodge and A/C rooms. Bar, restaurant, pool, tour desk. Pick up for all cruises and tours Nadi/Lautoka.
Price A$22-60 (US$14-39).

Sunseekers Hotel, Narewa Road,
ph 700 400, fax 702 047.
Includes a Youth Hostel. Coffee shop, pool, gift shop, restaurant, bar, tour desk. Dormitory rates include free continental breakfast. Other rooms self-contained with fan or A/C.
**Price single A$25 (US$16), double A$30 (US$19),
dorm A$6 (US$4).**

Whitehouse Inn, PO Box 174, Nadi,
ph 700 022.
For budget travellers. Cooking facilities, tea and coffee making, laundry, ironing, pool, A/C or fan cooled rooms fully serviced. Tour desk. Near golf course, 5 minutes from Nadi shopping. Courtesy transport to and from airport.
Price A$20-30 (US$13-20), dorm $8 (US$5).

Nadi Area Resorts

Sheraton Fiji Resort, PO Box 9761, Nadi Airport,
ph 750 777, fax 750 818.
On Denerau Beach, 20 minutes from Nadi Airport, 10 minutes from Nadi town, near departure point for daily launch to Mamanuca Islands and the Island Hopper Helipad. 300 rooms all with ocean views. Daily children's activities, pool, creche, babysitting, children's menu, evening bbq. 4 restaurants, bars. Free activities: windsurfing, catamarans, laser cars, volleyball, aerobics, daytime tennis. Other activities: Golf, waterskiing, new health club, scuba diving, snorkelling trips, sunset cruise, night tennis, deep-sea fishing, local and off-shore excursions. Cultural activities: woodcarving, storytelling, garden walk tour, Kava and torch lighting ceremony, Meke and firewalking show, fashion shows.
Price twin share A$160-350 (US$104-228), single A$310-699 (US$202-454).

Sheraton Royal Denarau Resort, PO Box 9081, Nadi Airport,
ph 750 000, fax 750 259.
Next door to the Sheraton Fiji and the facilities of both hotels can be used. 276 rooms, 3 handicapped rooms, 6 suites. Children's menus, children's playground, activities, babysitting, pool. Meal guide: 3 meals a day around A$80 (US$56) with a choice of 4 restaurants and bars.
Free activities: daytime court use at tennis club, hobic cats, windsurfing, paddle boats, lawn bowls, archery, mini golf,

aerobics, volleyball, games bure. Other activities: golf, tennis lessons, waterskiing, parasailing, scuba diving, snorkelling expeditions, deep-sea fishing, daily full day and half day tours and cruises, sunset cruise.

Cultural activities: Denarau Village - living arts complex with carving, weaving, pottery and garland making, traditional meke, firewalking.

Price twin share A$111-323 (US$72-210), single A$222-646 (US$144-420).

Sonaisali Island Resort, PO Box 2544, Nadi,
ph 706 011, fax 720 411.
10km south of Nadi Airport, 10 minutes from Nadi town. Built on a large island 300m from mainland with sheltered lagoon and water sports. 32 rooms and 6 bures. Rooms have one king or 2 queen beds. Bures have 2 bedrooms (1 air-conditioned) 1 queen, 1 double sofa, 2 single beds. Child menus, babysitting, playground, kids pool. Stay 7 nights pay for 6 and receive free jungle cruise per person. This is a superior resort with good facilities, yet accessible to Nadi town and attractions.

Price suite twin share A$90 (US$58), single A$180 (US$117), child 2-15 free. Bure twin share $A158 (US$102), single A$316 (US$205).

Lautoka
Waterfront, Volivoli Road,
ph 664 777, fax 665 870.
On the waterfront 30 minutes from Nadi. 41 rooms with one double and one single bed. Convenient to Blue Lagoon Cruise departures, adjacent to Lautoka shops and business centre.

Price twin share A$48 (US$31), single A$95 (US$62).

Cathay Hotel, PO Box 239, Lautoka,
ph 660 566, fax 340 236.
46 rooms with fridge, tea/coffee making and phone. Licensed dining room, lounge, pool. Function room. Off street parking. Security.
Price A/C suite, sleeps 3, A$66 (US$43), A/C double and twins, private facilities A$44 (US$29), A/C single with private bath A$37 (US$24), doubles and twins with fans and bath A$30 (US$20), singles with fans and private baths A$26 (US$17), dormitory with bath and fans A$10 (US$6) per person.

Saweni Beach Hotel, PO Box 239, Lautoka, ph 661 777, fax 660 136.
14 self-contained beachfront apartments that sleep 3. All have fans and verandah. Licensed lounge and bar, mini market, pool, parking.
Price A$40-46 (US$26-30). Dormitory with fans A$10 per person (US$6).

Mamanuca Islands

These islands off Nadi have been transformed into holiday resorts. Wherever you stay the mood is the same. Don't worry about packing a lot of clothes, buy a Fijian sulu, which is their version of a sarong. Wear shoes for coral reefs. Swim, sail snorkel, watch the brightly coloured fish, look at coral through a glass-bottomed boat. Take a day cruise to another island.

Information on access to the islands is found in the Sightseeing chapter.

Plantation Island Resort, PO Box 9176, Nadi Airport,
ph 669 333, fax 669 200.
41 hotel-style rooms, 71 bures located 20km due west of Nadi. Access is by launch ($1^1/_2$ – 2 hours) or air (10 minutes). 2 restaurants, 3 bars, boutique, gift shop, games room, live entertainment, disco, babysitting available. Snorkelling, hand-line

fishing, sailing, canoes, wind -surfing, tennis, volleyball, bush-walking, table tennis and mini-golf. Extra activities include: water skiing, paragliding, banana boating, island hopping, coral viewing, shell village trip, tandem skydiving, scuba diving.
Price double/twin A$85-155 (US$55-100), single A$162-310 (US$105-202).

Mana Island Resort, PO Box 610, Lautoka,
ph 661 455, fax 650 788.
32 beachfront rooms and 128 bures located 17km west-north-west of Nadi. Access is by launch from Denarau (1<$E1/2> hours) or by helicopter/seaplane (10 minutes). 2 restaurants, 3 bars, coffee shop, 3 beaches, pool, gift shop, tennis, baby sitting. Activities include windsurfing, hobie cats, canoes, snorkelling, 2 tennis courts with lights, volleyball, table tennis, billiard table.
Price double/twin A$93-180 (US$60-117), single A$186-360 (US$120-234).

Naitasi Island Resort, PO Box 10044, Nadi Airport,
ph 669 999, fax 669 197.
28 bures and 10 villas with kitchen facilities situated 22km west-north-west of Nadi Bay on Malolo Island. Access is by launch from Nadi Bay (1½ – 2 hours), seaplane (12 minutes) or helicopter (12 minutes). 2 restaurants, 2 bars, pool, nightly entertainment, boutique. Activities include sailing, paddle boards, windsurfing, canoes, fish feeding, coral viewing, snorkelling gear, half-court tennis, beach volley ball, nature and cultural walking trails, Fijian cultural demonstrations and Fijian cooking classes. Extra activities are scuba diving, sea kayaks, game fishing, water skiing, paraflying, jetskiing island hopping.
Price double/twin A$104-203 (US$68-132), single A$175-364 (US$123-255).

Treasure Island, PO Box 2210, Lautoka,
ph 666 999, fax 666 955.
Located 18km south-west of Nadi, access is by helicopter or seaplane from the airport (8 minutes), or by coach to either Lautoka or Denarau Marine (30 minutes), then an hour launch trip. 67 beachfront bures, snack bar, cocktail lounge, restaurant, pool, spa, boutique and gift shop, baby sitting. Activities include coral viewing, mini-golf, sailing, volleyball, hand-line fishing, windsurfing, cultural demonstrations and entertainment. Extra activities are game fishing, para sailing, scuba diving, water skiing, jet skiing and toboggan rides.
Price double/twin A$123-196 (US$80-127), single A$246 (US$160).

Beachcomber Island, PO Box 364, Lautoka,
ph 661 500, fax 664 496.
Located 18km south-west of Lautoka, access is by coach to Lautoka (20 minutes), then an hour launch trip. 20 private bures, 14 lodge-style rooms plus dormitory with 20 two-tier bunks. Activities include snorkelling, mini golf, coral viewing, volley ball, nightly entertainment, four cultural shows weekly. Extra activities are paddle boats, fishing trips, windsurfing, scuba diving/training, water skiing, island tours, parasailing, giant toboggan, jet skis.
Price lodge (shared facilities) A$83 (US$54), bure (private facilities) A$113 (US$73) per person. All meals are included.

Tokoriki Island Resort, PO 9729, Nadi Airport,
ph 661 999, fax 665 295.
Located 29km west-north-west of Nadi, access is by launch to Mana Island ($1^1/_2$ hours), then 30 minutes by speedboat, or 12 minutes from Nadi Bay to Mana Island by seaplane, or 15 minutes direct to Tokoriki by helicopter. 19 beach front bures, 2 restaurants, bars, pool and spa, resort shop, games room and evening entertainment. Activities include volleyball, bush walking,

snorkelling, water skiing, windsurfing, kayaking, fishing, hobie cats, barbecues, mekes, shuttle service to Matamanoa. Extra charge for scuba diving.

Price twin A$133-155 (US$86-100), single A$265-310 (US$172-201). Meals F$61 adult, F$28 child (payable on arrival) consist of continental breakfast, a la carte lunch, set menu 3 course dinner.

Matamanoa Island Resort, PO Box 9729, Nadi Airport,
ph 723 620, fax 720 282.
Located 28km west-north-west of Nadi, access if by launch (1$\frac{1}{2}$ hours) or air (12 minutes) from Nadi Bay to Mana Island, then 30 minutes by speedboat to Matamanoa, or by helicopter direct to Matamanoa (15 minutes). 20 bures with ocean views and 4 garden rooms, restaurant, bar, pool, tennis and entertainment. Activities include sailing, windsurfing, fishing, coral viewing, snorkelling, paddle boards, tennis, indoor games and banana boats. Extra activities are sport fishing, water skiing, scuba diving and island trips.

Price garden room twin A$69 (US$45), single A$138 (US$90); bures twin A$118 (US$77), single A$236 (US$153).

Castaway Island Resort, Private Mail Bag, Nadi Airport,
ph 661 233, fax 665 753.
Located 24km west-north-west of Nadi, access is by launch (1$\frac{1}{2}$ – 2 hours) or by seaplane or helicopter (10-12 minutes). 66 bures, cocktail and casual bars and open-air dining. Activities include scuba lesson, snorkelling, glass bottom boat coral viewing, volleyball, indoor games, tennis and equipment (all weather and floodlit), windsurfing, sailing, paddle boats and canoes, traditional entertainment. Extra activities are scuba training and diving, sport fishing, jetskiing and parasailing.

Price, which includes full buffet breakfast, twin A$134-302 (US$87-196), single A$267-604 (US$173-393).

Musket Cove Resort, Private Mail Bag, Nadi Airport,
ph 722 488, Island 662 878, fax 720 378, Island 662 633.
Located on Malololailai Island, 15km west of Nadi, and accessed by a ten minute flight. Choice of beachfront, seaview and garden bures or luxury units. Restaurant, barbecue, 2 bars, entertainment, supermarket, boutique, pool, baby sitting. Activities include snorkelling, bush walks, water skiing, windsurfing, rowboats, canoes and line-fishing. Extra activities are deep sea sports or game fishing, scuba diving with PADI instruction facility, hobie cats, daily yacht cruises, day trips.
Price twin A$100-150 (US$65-97), single A$200-300 (US$130-195).

Vomo Island

Sheraton Vomo Resort, PO Box 5650, Lautoka,
ph 667 955, fax 667 997.
Located 15 minutes by jet helicopter from Nadi Airport, the resort has 30 luxurious villas, 3 restaurants, 2 bars, pool, poolside snacking, boutique, Fijian serenaders. Activities include catamarans, windsurfing, golf driving range, Pitch 'n Putt golf, tennis, croquet, snorkelling, exercise circuit, arts & crafts demonstrations, surf skiing. Extra activities include water skiing, scuba diving, deep sea fishing, golf at Denarau with helicopter transfers, cruises, traditional ceremonies and guided adventure treks.
Price (min. 3 night stay) twin/single A$435-495 (US$282-320), including all meals.

Yasawa Island

The island is the most northerly of the Yasawa Group, and is about 50km north-west of Nadi. Access is by a Sunflower Airlines 30 minute scenic flight.

Yasawa Island Resort, PO Box 10128, Nadi Airport,
ph 663 364, fax 665 044.
16 one and two-bedroom bures and villas. All meals and activities

are included, except scuba diving and light tackle fishing. Restaurant, bar, casual entertainment, mekes (Fijian dancing) and lovos (feasts), pool and tennis court.

Prices start from A$350 (US$228) per double, and transfers are extra, but all meals are included.

Coral Coast

Shangri-la's Fijian Resort. Private Mail Bag Nadi International Airport,
ph 528 720, fax 500 402
84 rooms on Ocean, 48 on Reef, 101 Lagoon Superior, 44 Coral superior, 22 Coral family rooms, 48 Golden Cowrie, 66 Lagoon deluxe, 7 studios, 20 suites and 4 beach bures. 5 restaurants, pool, 9-hole golf course, 7 cocktail bars, disco, daily movies, safe swimming beach, children's pool, daily children's programs, free child care centre for 1-6, plus baby sitting.

Plenty of activities for singles. Free activities and facilities: 9-hole golf course, 5 tennis courts, lawn bowls, handline fishing competition, sailing dinghies, canoeing, snorkelling gear, windsurfing, croquet, aerobics, volleyball, badminton, indoor games, in-house movies.

Other activities: scuba diving, deep-sea fishing, snorkelling safari, private golf and tennis lessons, firewalking, waterskiing. Free: traditional meke, kava drinking, torch lighting ceremony. There is also a full range of day trips and excursions available from the tour desk.

Price: twin share A$114-349 (US$57-227), single A$230-700 (US$150-455).

The Warwick, PO Box 100, Korolevu,
ph 530 555, fax 530 010.
On the beach, $2^1/_2$ hours from Nadi Airport by coach, $1^1/_2$ hours by car. Set on leafy gardens on a long white beach. 250 mountain and ocean view rooms, 23 Warwick Club rooms, 10 suites, each with one double and one sofa bed. Children's menus, playground and

activities, indoor games and amusement machines, babysitting, child care centre.

Free activities: windsurfing, canoes, snorkelling, kayaks, 6 hole pitch'n'putt golf, volleyball, scuba lesson, live entertainment and lots more. Extra activities, scuba diving, horseback riding, coral viewing, deep sea fishing, squash, waterfall hikes, firewalking, day tours and excursions, floodlit tennis. Well established popular hotel. You can use the facilities of The Naviti Hotel.

Price twin share A$64-177 (US$42-115), single A$128-354 (US$83-230), child 2-15 free.

The Naviti, PO Box 29, Korolevu,
ph 530 444, fax 530 343.
Situated on a sandy lagoon $2^1/_2$ hours by coach, $1^1/_2$ hours by car from Nadi Airport. Set in large open grounds surrounded by hills. 32 mountain view, 108 ocean view rooms, 4 suites with one queen bed, plus rollaway if required. Children's menu and meal sittings, activities and donkey rides, babysitting, children's pool, playground and nanny service.

Free activities: snorkel gear, windsurfing, canoes, tennis, golf, paddle skis, scuba diving lesson, volley ball, village tour, evening entertainment, games room, TV room.

Extra activities: horseback riding, coral viewing, snorkelling, fishing trips, firewalking.

Price twin share A$64-153 (US$42-99), single A$126-305 (US$82-198), child 2-15 free. An 'All Inclusive plan costs twin A$137-192 (US$89-125), single A$190-373 (US$124-242) and includes all meals with unlimited wine and beer with main meals, unlimited access to Kids Fun Park, Kids Club and many sporting activities.

The Reef Resort, PO Box 173, Sigatoka,
ph 500 044, fax 520 074.
On the beach in the heart of the Coral Coast $1^1/_2$ hours by coach, 70 minutes by car from Nadi Airport. 68 rooms, 5 family rooms

with one queen bed and one single. Babysitting, cots, highchairs, children's menu and meal times, kids pool, playground, supervised kids activities.
Free activities: tennis, games room, horseriding, bicycles, canoes, fishing, reef walking, snorkelling, one scuba dive lesson. Near Sigatoka for shopping.
Price twin share A\$66 (US\$43), single A\$135 (US\$88). Family room A\$85 (US\$55), child 2-15 free. Meal guide: for a minimum of 7 nights you can purchase a 'Reef Feast' meal package for A\$76 (US\$50) per adult, A\$53 (US\$34) per child under 12.

Hideaway Resort, PO Box 233, Sigatoka,
ph 500 177, fax 520 025.
On sandy beach 2 hours by coach from Nadi Airport, 70 minutes by car. Ocean swimming at high tide only. Leafy gardens. 56 deluxe and 2 bedroom bures. Baby sitters, cots, highchairs, children's pool, playground, supervised activities and bumper boats.
Free activities: windsurfing, snorkelling, tennis, volleyball, bicycles, golf driving range, archery, mini golf, nightly entertainment, one scuba diving lesson.
Price twin share A\$65 (US\$42), single A\$126 (US\$82), air conditioned bure \$162 (US\$105), child 2-15 free. Meal guide: Hideaway's 'Magic Pass' (min. 5 nights stay) includes five cooked breakfasts and five special lunches, plus one day unlimited kilometre car hire (category A) for A\$110 (US\$77) each.

Centra Pacific Harbour, PO Box 144, Deuba,
ph 450 022, fax 450 262.
On long sandy beach 3$^1/_2$ hours by coach, 2$^1/_2$ hours by car from Nadi Airport. Near the Cultural Centre and Marketplace of Fiji. 84 rooms with twin or double bed plus up to 2 rollaways. Babysitters, high chairs, cots, children's menus, playground facilities, children's pool.

Free activities: canoes, tennis, turtle feeding, volleyball, snorkelling, games room.

Extra activities: golf, deep-sea fishing, sailing, scuba diving, windsurfing, waterskiing, fire walking (Tuesday/ Saturday) horseriding. Only 40 minutes from Suva.

Price twin share A$80 (US$52), single A$160 (US$104), child 2-15 free.

Tambua Sands Beach Resort, PO Box 177, Sigatoka, **ph 500 399, fax 520 265.**
25 bures and 6 rooms situated about $1^{1}/_{4}$ hours from Nadi Airport. Facilities include swimming pool, bar and restaurant, boutique, live entertainment, disco and baby sitting.

Free activities: Volleyball, table tennis, reef walking and traditional song and dance performances.

Extra activities: snorkelling tours, horseriding, village & plantation visits, beach picnic with lovo lunch, fishing, snorkelling, tours, cruises and shopping tours.

Price double A$50 (US$32), single A$95 (US$62).

Vakaviti Resort, PO Box 5, Sigatoka,
ph 500 526, fax 520 319.
6 self-contained lagoon-side bures in tropical garden. Walking distance to restaurants and entertainment. Snorkelling, scuba diving. Restful holiday.
Price double/twin A$50 (US$32), single A$40 (US$26), dormitory A$12 (US$8).

Vatulele Island

Vatulele is about 48km south of Korolevu on Viti Levu, and can be reached by Sunflower Airlines flights from Nadi Airport. The trip takes 25 minutes. The price of staying here includes accommodation, all activities (excluding scuba diving and sport fishing), all meals and all drinks including wines and French champagne. 15 villas, complete with wet bar, and activities include swimming, snorkelling, jungle hikes, bocce ball, volleyball, hand-line fishing and tennis. Min. 4 nights stay. Children under 12 years are only permitted to stay on designated family weeks.
Price double/twin A$2850 (US$1852), single A$3350 (US$2177). Bookings for this resort can be made through their office in Sydney, Australia - PO Box 470, Woollahra, 2025,
ph (02) 9326 1055, fax (02) 9327 2764.

Suva

Suva Travelodge, PO Box 1357,
ph 301 600, fax 300 251.
On waterfront close to all activities. 130 rooms with one queen and one single bed. All facilities expected of a Travelodge. Close to shops and restaurants.
Price twin share A$58 (US$37), single A$115 (US$75), child 2-15 free.

Raffles Tradewinds, PO Box 3377, Lami, Suva,
ph 362 450, fax 362 455.
10 minutes from Suva overlooking 'Bay of Islands' at Lami. 108 rooms with queen or king size beds. New York deli/brasserie and floating chargrill restaurant.
Price twin share A$56 (US$36), single A$99 (US$64), child 2-15 free.

Suva Peninsula Hotel, PO Box 888, Suva,
ph 313 711, 313 574, fax 314 473.
40 A/C units (standard, deluxe and family) only 5 minutes from GPO. Lounge/bar, restaurant, lift, pool, parking, function hall.
Price double/twin from A$80 (US$52), single from A$60 (US$39).

Capricorn Apartment Hotel, 7-11 Forte Street (PO Box 1261), Suva,
ph 303 732, fax 303 069.
In the heart of Suva City with one of the best views of the city and the harbour. 3 hour drive from Nadi airport. Studio and 1 or 2 bedroom apartments. Swimming pool, restaurants nearby.
Prices A$80 (US$52) to A$105 (US$68).

South Seas Private Hotel, PO Box 2086, Government Buildings, Suva,
ph 312 296, fax 340 236.
All rooms have fans and insect screens. Communal bathroom and kitchen. Washing facilities. Security. Short walk to city.
Price double/twin A$9 (US$6) per person, singles A$11 (US$7), family units A$26 (US$17).

Toberua Island

The 1.6ha island is off the east coast of Viti Levu about 1 hour by car and launch from Suva. The resort is of first class standard. 14 large bures. Children's menus, cots, highchairs, babysitting.

Free activities: windsurfing, paddle-boats, sailing, canoes, water-skiing, snorkelling, table tennis, reef golf. Very up-market and member of the Select Hotel Group.

Price twin share A$145 (US$94), single A$265 (US$172). Compulsory Meal Plan - 3 meals daily cost adult F$87, child 2-15 F$41, payable on arrival.

Ovalau Island

Leleuvia Island Resort, GPO Box 14810, Suva,
ph 313 366 (island ph 301 584).

Situated on a 17ha island off Ovalau. 3 dormitories, 15 bures, canteen, dining hall, volleyball, snorkelling, scuba diving and fishing. Close to Levuka. For backpackers.

Price bungalows A$26 (US$17), bure A$21 (US$14), dorm A$18 (US$12), tent A$15 (US$10). All prices include 3 meals.

Naigani Island

Naigani Island Resort, GPO Box 12359, Suva,
ph 312 069, fax 302 058.

Off the north-east coast of Viti Levu. A one hour scenic drive through villages from Suva then a 30 minute cruise to the 218.52ha beach-fringed island of Naigani. Moderate class. 9 large deluxe 2 bedroom villas and 3 three bedroom deluxe villas. Each sleep 6-8 people. Children's activities, special meals, babysitting. Meal plan must be purchased on arrival and paid for in local currency, adult F$38.50, child up to 11 years F$19.25 for 3 meals a day.

Free activities: snorkelling, windsurfing, canoeing, hand-line fishing, bush walks. Formerly Mystery Island, Naigani is steeped in history. Nearby Levuka, Fiji's old capital, can be reached by boat. Ideal for families.

Price A$120 (US$78) per villa (sleeps 6).

Rakiraki

Rakiraki Hotel, PO Box 31, Rakiraki,
ph 694 101, fax 694 545.

On the north-east side of Viti Levu, $2^1/_2$ hour drive from Nadi. 36 rooms with one double and one single bed. In part of Fiji not usually seen by tourists. Colonial style hotel set in garden. Lawn bowls. Quaint charming atmosphere.

Price, with air conditioning, A$45-50 (US$29-32).

Nanunu-I-Ra

Mokusigas Island Resort, 130km north-east of Nadi Airport on the island of Nananu-i-ra, just off the coast of Rakiraki,
ph 694 449, 694 404.

2 hours by car or coach from Nadi to Rakiraki, then 10 minutes by launch to the 870 acre island with 7 white sandy beaches surrounded by clear water and reefs. Moderate class. 14 Laguna Vista and 6 Ocean Panorama bures. Recommended as an adult resort but children over 7 years can be catered for. Meal Guide: F$58 per adult, F$29 per child for 3 meals a day.

Free activities: snorkelling, windsurfing, gymnasium, tennis, volleyball, surf skis, nature walks.
Price twin share A$100-143 (US$65-93), single A$204-285 (US$132-185).

Wananavu Beach Resort, Volivoli Road, Rakiraki,
ph 694 433, fax 694 499.
There are 12 bures and 2 x 8 bed dorms, and facilities include restaurants, 2 bars, entertainment, pool, boutique and baby sitting. Activities are snorkelling, scuba diving, water skiing, fishing, canoes, tennis court, paddleboards, island picnic trips, village trips, horse riding.
Price, including cooked breakfast, double A$85 (US$55), single A$170 (US$110). Meal plans are available at A$35 (US$23).

Vanua Levu
Kontiki Resort, Private Mail Bag, Savusavu,
ph 850 262, fax 850 355.
15 minutes from Savusavu airport on Vanua Lavu. 60.7 hectares of copra, bananas, pineapples, pawpaws, across the road from the beach. Budget class. 13 bures, 1 family bure, 1 suite, 1 honeymoon bure. Babysitting, children's playground.
Free activities: golf, tennis, snorkelling, reef walks, bush hikes, volleyball, croquet. Other activities: scuba diving, fishing.
Price A$105-225 (US$68-146).

Cousteau Island Resort is on the southern shore of Vanua Levu, 3 miles from Savusavu,
ph 850 188, fax 850 340.
Operated by Jean Michel Cousteau and the creators of Post Ranch Inn in Big Sur, California. The 20 bures are set in 6.8ha of coconut grove, and facilities are open-air restaurant, bar, entertainment, pool, marine biologist on site, massage, Cousteau Kids Program and baby sitting. Activities include excursions and educational

programs, marine science lectures, rainforest hikes, kayaking, snorkelling, sailing and telescopic stargazing. Scuba diving is also available.

Price, which includes all meals, twin A$224-322 (US$146-209), single A$295-643 (US$192-418).

Namale Resort, PO Box 244, Savusavu,
ph 850 435, fax 850 400.

Set on a peninsula surrounded by white sandy beach, a coral reef and a rainforest, the resort has 10 bures catering for a maximum of 20 guests, restaurants, bar and lounge, pool, jacuzzi. Activities include snorkelling, sailing, windsurfing, banana boats, sea kayaks, fishing, tennis, horse riding, basketball, volleyball, badminton. Extra activities are daily guided tours of local villages, coconut plantation, reef and jungle waterfall and scuba diving. Children over 12 accepted, but not encouraged.

Price, which includes all meals and all alcoholic and other drinks, twin A$427 (US$277), single A$710 (US$462).

Taveuni

Taveuni, the Garden Isle of Fiji, is a $1^1/_2$ hour flight from Nadi by Sunflower Airlines. It is a combination of a romantic past and an unspoiled present. Breathtaking excursions are available: 4WD to Tagimoucia Crater Lake, bird watching, 40m Bouma Cascade waterfall, and world-renowned dive sites.

Qamea Beach Club, PO Matei, Taveuni,
ph 880 220, fax 880 092.
Off the island of Taveuni. $1^1/_2$ hours by Sunflower Airlines from Nadito Taveuni Airport then 30 minutes by taxi and boat to the island. First class right on the beach. 11 luxurious Fijian bures. Children under 13 not accepted. 3 meals a day cost F$116. This is compulsory and paid on arrival.
Free activities: windsurfing, village tours, outriggers, snorkelling, dinghies. An upmarket resort well away from the tourist run.
Price twin share A$180 (US$117), single A$350 (US$227). Return vehicle/boat transfers from Taveuni Airport cost A$110 (US$71) per person.

Garden Island Resort, PO Box 1, Waiyevo, Taveuni,
ph 880 286, fax 880 288.
A half-hour drive from Taveuni Airport, Garden Island is renowned for its friendliness, great cuisine, and value for money. There are 30 guest rooms with ocean views, and facilities include restaurant, bar/lounge, pool and dive centre. Activities are paddle boats, table tennis, natural rock water slide nearby, and a walk to the international date line. Extra activities are scuba diving, snorkelling, scenic island tours to waterfalls and villages, and canoeing.
Price single A$55 (US$36), dormitory A$18 (US$12).

Maravu Plantation Resort, c/- Postal Agency, Matei, Taveuni,
ph 880 555, fax 880 600.
On the island of Taveuni, 150m from beach in a copra plantation. 3 honeymoon, 7 deluxe bures. Babysitting, cots, children's meals. Excellent "Wananavu" Restaurant and bar. Specialises in eco-tours.
Price share twin A$153 (US$99), single A$247 (US$160).

Nukubati Island
The island is less than a kilometre off the north coast of Vanua Levu, and one hour by boat from Labasa, Vanua Levu's largest town. The very up-market resort caters for eight guests (four couples, no children) in four luxury bures. Facilities include restaurant, bar, library, lounge, pavilion, barbecue area and remote dining locations. The address is PO Box 1928 Labasa,
ph 813 901, fax 813 914.
Activities include sailing, windsurfing, snorkelling, coral viewing, fishing, nature walks, golf, tennis and lawn bowls. Extra activities include big game fishing, off-shore cruising and scuba diving on the sea reef.
Price (which includes all meals and non-alcoholic drinks) A$300 (US$195) per person.

CRUISES

Blue Lagoon Cruises, PO Box 130, Lautoka.
ph 661 622, fax 664 098,
The best known of the cruise operators. They have a fleet of six modern motor yachts that accommodate up to 40 passengers, and cruise through the Yasawa and Mamanuca Islands. Cabins are two or three berth, are air-conditioned, and have private facilities.
Cruise options are:
3 days/2 nights Lycianda Cruise -
share twin A$620-734 (US$403-477).
4 days/3 nights Yasawa Princess Cruise -
share twin A$899-1106 (US$584-719).
7 days/6 nights Nanuya Princess Cruise -
share twin A1613-1944 (US$1048-1263).
4 days/3 nights Mystique Princess Cruise -
share twin A1334-1768 (US$867-1149).

Captain Cook Cruises, PO Box 23, Nadi,
ph 701 823, fax 702 045,
offer trips on a motor cruiser that can carry 1200 passengers. The 4 days/3 nights cruise around the Mamanuca and southern Yasawa Islands, costs **A$791-1031 (US$514-670)** which includes accommodation, meals and watersports, except for scuba diving which is an added expense.

The 5 days/4 nights sailing safaris visit the Yasawa Islands and cost **A$1063-1378 (US$690-895)** which includes meals and all activities, except scuba diving.

The Combined Cruise lasts 8 days/7 nights, and includes both the above, plus a day in Nadi between cruises.
It costs A$1493-1956 (US$970-1270).

LOCAL TRANSPORT

Air

Air Pacific, the international carrier, has several flights daily from Nadi to Nausori Airport, near Suva. The airline has offices at Nadi International Airport,
ph 720 888, and on Victoria Parade in Suva, ph 304 388.

Air Fiji flies out of Nausori Airport, and has more domestic flights than its opposition Sunflower Airlines, which flies out of Nadi. Every island that has tourist accommodation can be reached by air, and other islands have serviced airstrips, but don't think that you can just drop in uninvited. It is necessary to be invited to a non-tourist island, or at least to seek permission from authorities.
Air Fiji's head office is in Victoria Parade, Suva,
ph 313 666, fax 300 771, and they have another office at Nadi Airport, **ph 722 521.**

Sunflower Airlines' main office is at Nadi Airport,
ph 723 016, fax 720 085, and they have another in Pier Street, Suva, **ph 315 755. Travellers should be warned that the planes flown by this airline carry a maximum of around 20 passengers - not your normal jumbo jet by any means.** If small planes are not on your thrill list, it would be better to think of getting to your resort island by boat.

Turtle Airways, Private Mail Bag, Nadi Airport,
ph 722 389, fax 722 988, have 5 Cessna 206 flyplanes, which take 4 passengers and their luggage (15kg per person), and operate sunrise to sunset. They depart from the seaplane base, Nadi Bay, and rates are Island Resorts **A$90 (US$63)** per person, Charter flights **A$650 (US$455)** per hour, Scenic flights - 10 minutes **A$49 (US$35)** per person, 30 minutes **A$100 (US$70)** per person.

Island Hoppers offer transfers to island and mainland resorts,
ph 790 410, fax 790 172.

Bus

There are plenty of local buses especially around the towns. The charges are reasonable, ranging around 40c-55c. Buses can usually be waved down from the side of the road. This is one way, of course, to experience the real Fiji, but I think that visiting a village is much better. Timetables, if they exist, are ignored, and even short trips on local buses can take hours. They are social occasions, and it is not unusual for the driver to have a long chat with someone who is getting off the bus, holding everybody else in limbo until he is ready to get going again.

Air-conditioned coaches are available to take tourists on excursions. Passengers on package deals are met at the airport by their hotel or tour operator.

Taxis

Most towns have taxi services. All taxis are metered and the fares are reasonable, 50c flag fall during and day and $1 after 10pm, plus 10c per kilometre. If making a longer trip by taxi, agree a price before you start.

Car

Overseas driving licences and international permits are recognised for six months after arrival. The minimum age limit for driving is 21 and the maximum 65. Driving is on the left hand side of the road, although in the small towns and villages the locals tend to drive in the middle of the road, and it seems they also consider the most important part of a car to be the horn, which they use frequently.

All major car rental firms operate in Fiji and can be booked before you leave, at the airport or from your hotel.

Avis, **ph 313 833** (Suva), **ph 722 233** (Nadi Airport).

Budget, **ph 315 899** (Suva), **ph 722 735** (Nadi Airport).

Central, **ph 311 866** (Suva), **ph 722 771** (Nadi Airport), **ph 664 511** (Lautoka).

Dove, ph **311 755** (Suva), **ph 721 606** (Nadi).

Hertz, **ph 302 186** (Suva), **ph 723 466** (Nadi).

Khan's, **ph 385 033** (Suva), **ph 701 009** (Nadi Town), **ph 723 506** (Nadi Airport).

Thrifty, **ph 314 436** (Suva), **ph 722 935** (Nadi Airport).

Sharmas, **ph 314 365** (Suva), **ph 721 908** (Nadi Airport).

Roxy Rentals, **ph 722 763** (Nadi Airport).

Sea

Regular services run between the major islands, but it is not the quickest way to travel. The ferries carry freight as well as passengers, and the few available cabins are on a first-come-first-served basis.

Consort Shipping, Suva, **ph 302 877,** and Patterson Brothers, Suva, **ph 315 644,** run inter-island and car ferry services. Also contactable in Suva are Emosis Ferry Service, **ph 313 366,** and Whippys Ferry, **ph 340 015**.

The Island Express, run by South Sea Cruises, provides a twice daily service from Nadi to resorts in the Mamanuca Group, **ph 720 095.**

Beachcomber Cruises, **ph 661 500** (Lautoka), operate the hydrofoil Drodrolagi between Viti Levu and Vanua Levu Mon-Sat. It is wise to contact the Fiji Visitors Bureau and get their advice as to which company will best suit your needs.

EATING OUT

The resort hotels have a good variety of meals, usually with European, Fijian, Chinese and Indian cuisines being available. There are small cafes and restaurants in all major towns, for example, Chefs, Sangayam Road, Nadi, **ph 703 131** - open Mon-Sat for lunch 10am-2pm, candlelight dinner 6-10pm. Indian curry houses are plentiful. Chinese, Italian, French, European, Japanese and Fijian cuisine can be found, depending on the region. Contact the closest Information Centre for some suggestions as to where you can dine for a change.

On the outer islands, your resort or hotel may be the only restaurant available.

There are licensed restaurants, clubs and hotels throughout Fiji offering local beer, wines and spirits.

At hotels and resorts the prices are from:

Food - breakfast F$12; lunch F$16; dinner F$25.

Drinks - bottle of wine F$10; glass of beer F$5; cocktails from F$7.

At restaurants and pubs: dinner from F$10; glass of beer F$3.50 + 10% VAT, all payable in local currency.

Lovo

The 'lovo' is a Fijian feast in which food is wrapped in banana leaves and cooked slowly in an earth oven over smouldering stones. The food has a faintly smoked taste. Vegetables, meat, fish are placed in the earth oven. The centre piece is often a whole pig. This is a must.

ENTERTAINMENT

The larger towns have cinemas, nightclubs, and at weekends, dances. Ask your hotel what's on or check the local papers.
Movie tickets cost F$1.50 (US$0.99) (A$1.42);
Fijian Village entertainment F$24 (US$16) (A$23);
Hotel Island Night F$30 (US$20) (A$29).
Don't forget the 10% VAT.

SHOPPING

Fiji is a duty free shopping island. Duty free shops can be found in all towns and hotels. Check the local paper or the Fiji Visitors Bureau for a list. Everything from electrical goods to accessories can be found at reasonable prices. Resort wear and local fashions can be purchased in shops and resorts. These include sulus, bula shorts for men and swimwear. Tailors make quality men's and women's fashions in a few days. Dress lengths are an excellent buy. Bargaining is still conducted even in duty free shops. Fijian handicrafts are well made. Tapa, the name given to Fijian bark cloth, mats made from leaves, pottery, baskets and wood carving are all good buys.

SPORTS

Facilities for aquatic sports are found at all resorts. (Also see the Water Sports chapter.) Some also have para-flying. On-shore sports include tennis, volleyball (the staff and locals will join in with gusto), bowling, golf, archery, horse riding, aerobics, swimming and jogging. Team sports are cricket, soccer and rugby, and your hotel can arrange for you to watch an event.

Golf

18-hole courses
Denarau Golf and Racquet Club; Kontiki Resort; Nadi Airport Golf Club; Pacific Harbour Golf Club; Fiji Golf Club Suva.

9-hole courses
Ba Golf Club; Fiji Mocambo; Labasa Golf Club; Lautoka Golf Club; Rakiraki Golf Club; Reef Resort Golf Club; Fijian Shangri-la; The Naviti Golf Club; Vatukoula Golf Club.

Pitch'n'Putt

Warwick of Fiji; Sheraton Vomo; Regent of Fiji; Toberua Island Resort (only at low tide).

Sports events usually cost around F$10 (US$7).

Sightseeing

The Fiji Islands are a tropical paradise of white sandy beaches, coconut palms, clear blue water, and lagoons fringed with coral reefs. Larger islands have volcanic mountains, tropical rainforests, clear streams and waterfalls, but the birds and turtles prefer the smaller islands. Water sports, cruises and coral viewing from glass bottom boats are the main interests for visitors. The majority of resorts are found on Viti Levu the principal island where Suva and Nadi are situated. The resorts have everything anyone could need and many visitors spend their entire stay within the confines of their chosen accommodation. Others like to venture further afield, and this chapter is for them.

VITI LEVU

Fiji's main island, comprising 10,429 sq km, is home to the country's capital city, Suva, and many of Fiji's internationally renowned resorts and hotels. It is the primary location for the country's main industries of sugar, tourism, timber and gold, and most of the republic's population lives here. It has two deep water ports, Lautoka and Suva, two International Airports, Nadi and Nausori, and Fiji's greatest urban development at Suva, Nausori, Navua, Sigatoka, Nadi, Lautoka, Ba and Rakiraki.

A road follows the coastline around the island - it is called Queens Road from Nadi along the southern coast to Suva, and Kings Road from Suva along the northern coast to Nadi.

Nadi

Situated in the north-west of Viti Levu, Nadi (pronounced Nandee) is the site of Fiji's primary International Airport and the main point of entry for the majority of visitors.

During World War II, New Zealand forces converted a small airstrip into an operational Air Force base. When the war ended in 1945, the airstrip was developed to Civil Aviation standards, and became the first International Airport in Fiji, and an important stopover on north-south routes.

Nadi Town is the second largest city in Fiji, and is a ten-minute drive from the airport. It has a large market near the bus station, and there are many duty free shops to tempt visitors. This is the town's main business, and it has little else to offer. Strangely, though, Nadi has more hotels and resorts than any other centre in Fiji, and tourism is its main income earner.

At the southern end of town is the beautiful Sri Siva Subramaniya Hindu Temple. It is the largest in the Southern Hemisphere, and was built following designs that are thousands of years old.

Nearby, and joined by a causeway, is Denarau Island, home to luxury resorts, a championship golf course and a marina. Denarau is the starting point for cruises to the Mamanuca and Yasawa Islands, and is the home of Shotover Jet. This very exciting high speed boat departs every 30 minutes seven days a week to the islands.

Another place that attracts visitors is the Garden of the Sleeping Giant in Sabeto, a ten minute drive from town. The garden was developed by the late Raymond Burr (Perry Mason), in 1977, to house his collection of orchids. It has grown to the point of being the largest collection of orchids in Fiji, and exports to countries all over the world. The garden is open Mon-Sat 9am-5pm, and there is an admission fee.

The area around Nadi is farm country with sugar cane the main crop.

Lautoka

Situated 19km north of Nadi, Lautoka is the sugar capital of the country and has the largest mill. It is the main northern port, and sugar, timber and wood chip are exported from here.

The town is the departure point for the very popular Blue Lagoon Cruises, and has the biggest market in the country.

Although Lautoka has its fair share of duty free shops, it is more interested in sugar than tourism, and for that reason alone it is worth a visit. Besides, it is a very pretty little place.

The Mamanucas

The name is pronounced Mah-mah-noo-tha, this island group is in shallow waters off the western coast of Viti Levu. It is divided into two distinct areas, Mamanuca-i-Ra (leeward) and Mamanuca-i-Cake (windward), with the Malolo group to the south made up of Malolo, Qalito and Malololailai (the word lailai means 'little').

The area has had a violent history, although not all of it has been recorded. One example was in 1840 when a team of American explorers surrounded and destroyed the old Fijian villages of Arro (Yaro) and Sualib (Solevu) on the island of Malolo, and killed 57 villagers. This was in retaliation for the deaths of two American crewmen. Today visitors can see the site of the former villages, the graves of the two Americans, and the hill top where the villagers surrendered themselves and their homes to the American commander, Commodore Charles Wilkes, USN.

The Mamanuca group is now home to 12 resorts, and if visitors wish to visit a few resorts during their stay, staying in this vicinity might just be the way to do it.

How to get there
Access to the group, and between islands within it, can be by light aircraft, sea planes, helicopters, water taxis and cruise vessels.

The Yasawas
The westernmost islands of the Fijian chain, the Yasawas consist of 16 larger islands and ten small, including Yasawa, Waya, Naviti, Matacawalevu and Turtle Island, which 'starred' in the film Blue Lagoon.

The Dutch explorer Abel Tasman was the first to sight these islands when he was sailing around the area with two small ships, the Heemskerck and Flute Zeehaen, but he was hit by a storm near Nanuya, and never returned.

In 1774 Captain Cook sighted Turtle Island (Nanuya Levu), and in May 1789, Captain Bligh sailed into Yasawa waters in the longboat from the Bounty. American Commander Charles Wilkes surveyed and charted the group in 1840.

The islands owe some of their current fame to Blue Lagoon Cruises who make 4-7 day trips through them, but they also have magnificent mountain scenery, isolated beaches, and the limestone caves at Sawa-i-Lau. These have ancient writings on the wall that have archaeologists baffled. In all, well worth a visit.

How to get there
Access by boat can be arranged through the Lautoka Hotel, ph 660 388, fax 660 201, and the Cathay Hotel Lautoka, ph 660 566, fax 660 136. Return fares are around F$70 per person.

Sunflower Airline, **ph 723 016, fax 723 611,** and

Turtle Airways, **ph 722 389, fax 722 988,** have flights to the Yasawas.

The Coral Coast
The Coral Coast stretches from Yanuca, just outside Nadi Town, to Naboutini, which is approximately 80km from Suva. The area is blessed with white sand beaches, amazingly blue water, protective

reef, and some of the most expensive and most popular resorts in the country. There are two ways of visiting the Coral Coast if you have accommodation elsewhere - drive yourself, or take the local bus. Obviously, it is very convenient to have your own transport, but a trip on the local bus, stopping at little villages along the way, can be a very enjoyable experience. Allow plenty of time, though, no one on these buses ever seems to be in a hurry.

An attraction in this vicinity is the Coral Coast Railway, which travels from the Fijian Resort to the beautiful sandy Natadola Beach, passing through cane fields, rainforest and villages. There are many organised tours for this a 1911 steam train ride that include lunch and refreshments (see Tours).

Sigatoka

Sigatoka lies at the mouth of the Sigatoka River, Fiji's second longest river, in a fertile valley known as 'the salad bowl of Fiji'. It is a small town with a good market and duty free shops. It is much more pleasant shopping here than at Suva or Nadi.

Sigatoka Sand Dunes are a small, arid desert amidst the surrounding tropical vegetation, near Kulukulu village. Important archaeological relics have been found here establishing that Fiji was settled about 3500 years ago. The dunes begin at the mouth of the Sigatoka River and can be reached by a feeder road off the main Queen's Highway. Do not remove or 'souvenir' anything. Admission is free, **ph 315 944.**

Tavuni Hill Fort, radio ph RP 3740. Situated 4km off the main highway at Sigatoka, the Tavuni Hill fortification is an example of bygone eras. The site was manned by Tongan warriors whose descendants live in a village nearby and provide the guides to explain the history. Lookout points offer spectacular views. There is a reception bure with a display by the Fiji Museum. Refreshments, gift shop and toilets. Admission is F$6.

Pacific Harbour

This luxurious resort is situated a 40 minute drive from Suva, on the Coral Coast. Home of the mythical sharkgod, *Qaraniqio,* it is guarded by two female spirits. They had to be appeased before the swamps could be drained and the project commenced.

It has everything including a golf course and a five mile beach. Visit the Cultural Centre which is also the home of the Fiji Dance Theatre, and there watch craftsmen, musicians and artists at work. Pacific Harbour can also be reached on a day tour from Nadi.

Suva

The capital of Fiji is in the south-eastern corner of Viti Levu, and is very much a multi-racial town. It is well known for its duty free shopping, and the Municipal Market, where the locals buy their foodstuffs, is the liveliest in the South Pacific.

Suva became the capital in 1882 replacing Levuka, on the island of Ovalau. Its rapid growth through the establishment of trading companies, missionary churches and colonial government has given it many imposing buildings that date from the turn of the century. They are all protected under the Suva City Town Planning Scheme.

Walking Tour

A one hour walk from the heart of the city along Victoria Parade, following the foreshores, will reveal a variety of Fiji's most important buildings. Even when on this main street, watch out for touts. If someone asks your name, just ignore them, for if you tell them you will be presented with a wooden 'sword' with your name scratched on it, and be asked to pay some ridiculous price for it. Although this practice is not strictly illegal, it is frowned upon by local authorities, and you are under no obligation to buy.

Burns Philp, built in 1930, on Marks Road, was the first building in Suva to have a lift. Its large imposing design with central tower has been copied throughout the Pacific.

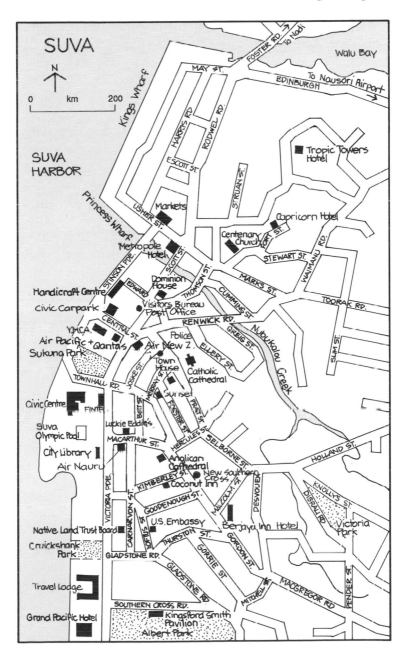

SUVA

N

0   km   200

SUVA HARBOR

Kings Wharf

Princess Wharf

Walu Bay

To Nadi

Foster Rd.

May St.

To Nausori Airport

Edinburgh

Harris Rd.

Rodwel Rd.

Escott St.

Struan St.

Tropic Towers Hotel

Usher St.

Markets

Capricorn Hotel

Centenary Church Rd.

Stewart St.

Waimanu Rd.

Toorak Rd.

Metropole Hotel

Scott St.

Thomson St.

Marks St.

Stinson Pde.

Edward

Dominion House

Handicraft Centre

Civic Carpark

Visitors Bureau
Post Office

Cumming St.

Renwick Rd.

Greig St.

Nubukalou Creek

Slum St.

YMCA

Central St.

Police

Air Pacific + Qantas

Air New Z.

Ellery St.

Sukuna Park

Joske St.

Town House

Catholic Cathedral

Townhall Rd.

Brett St.

Murray St.

Sunset

Foster St.

Pratt St.

Civic Centre

FINTEL

Luckie Eddie's

Macarthur St.

Hercules St.

Selborne St.

Holland St.

Suva Olympic Pool

City Library

Air Nauru

Kimberley St.

Anglican Cathedral

New Southern Cross

Coconut Inn

Malcolm St.

Desvoeux

Knolly's St.

Victoria Pde.

Carnarvon St.

Goodenough St.

Disraeli Rd.

Victoria Park

Native Land Trust Board

U.S. Embassy

Loftus St.

Thurston St.

Berjaya Inn Hotel

Cruickshank Park

Gladstone Rd.

Gladstone Rd.

Gorrie St.

Gordon St.

Macgregor Rd.

Pender St.

Travel Lodge

Southern Cross Rd.

Mitchell St.

Grand Pacific Hotel

Kingsford Smith Pavilion

Albert Park

Morris Hedstrom, originally Henry Marks, of the present Morris Hedstrom Supermarket and Department store chain, erected the building in 1918. It is situated on land once owned by large business concerns Brown & Joskie and Jung King Loon at the turn of the century. The arcaded verandah gives the building a Venetian appearance.

The **Fiji Visitors Bureau** in Thomson Street, occupies a Victorian building, erected in 1912 as a savings bank and telephone exchange.

Close by, **Sichuan Pavilion** restaurant and the **Garrick Hotel** date from 1920. Formally the Pier Hotel, built by the Costello family, it retains its original post-supported verandah and elaborate second story balcony.

Continue along Thomson Street to **G.B. Hari,** which was built around the start of World War I; it was formerly the Universal Picture Theatre. It is one of the few double storey wood and corrugated iron buildings remaining and has several shops on the ground floor and offices above.

The **Catholic Cathedral** is in Pratt Street. Father Rosier designed the crypt and nave in 1893. It was the initiative of Bishop Julian Vidal, Australian Bishop of Fiji. The pyrmont stones came from Hunters Hill, Sydney, and were carried in ships as ballast. The timber flooring came from Quebec, Canada.

Prouds Building on the corner of Thomson Street and Renwick Road was built by chemist Mitchelmore in 1929/31. This impressive three storey building faces the triangular park that was once the site of the original Suva market.

Fintel, on Victoria Parade, was built in 1926. The first radio broadcasts were made from a room in this building. It retains its cable and wireless function to this day.

A short distance along is the **Old Town Hall,** built in 1904 as a memorial to Queen Victoria on her Diamond Jubilee. With its cast iron lacework it is one of Suva's finest example of colonial architecture. In earlier times it was used by dance companies and for bazaars. **Suva City Library,** formally Carnegie Library, was built in 1909 with a grant from Andrew Carnegie. **St Andrew's**

Presbyterian Church in Gordon Street was built through the generosity of Mr William Kerr Thomson who donated 100 and the site. Built in 1883, it had just been finished when it was demolished by a hurricane. The present wooden church was erected in 1896. **Government Building,** built in 1939 on Victoria Parade, houses major government departments

Grand Pacific Hotel on Victoria Parade was designed to look like a ship, and opened in May 1914. All rooms were protected from the sun by wide verandahs and balconies. At present the building is being refurbished.

Albert Park has tennis courts, cricket grounds, parkland and a pavilion named after Charles Kingsford Smith, the Australian aviator. He made a rather spectacular landing here on June 6, 1928 on the second leg of his flight across the Pacific.

Botanic Gardens Clock Tower, further along Victoria Parade, was built in 1918 by Henry Marks & Co in memory of their director G.J. Mark, the first mayor of Suva. The tower is located in the Thurston Gardens, formerly called the Botanical Gardens. Close by is **Government House.** The original house, which was built on the site of an old Fijian village, **Nakorobaoa,** was destroyed by fire in March 1921. The new building was completed in 1928. The **Suva Museum,** also in Thurston Gardens, is open Mon-Thurs 8am-4.30pm, Fri 8am-4pm, Saturday 9am-4pm, and admission is F$3.30. It houses the most comprehensive collection of Fijian artifacts, and also offers tours on the Tabu Tabu-Soro, a traditional double-hulled canoe.

For those who do not wish to walk, because of the heat, there is a bus tour of Suva and surrounds, and enquiries can be made at the information office or your hotel.

Bau

A small island off Viti Levu, Bau lies a few kilometres south of Suva. It is the home of the Paramount Chief of Fiji, and also of the former Governor General Ratu Sir George Cakobau, whose grandfather ceded the Fiji Islands to Great Britain. To visit the island it is necessary to be invited by someone who lives there, or to obtain permission from the Ministry of Fijian Affairs. This rule is not just to keep tourists out, it also applies to native Fijians. Attractions that not many people get to see include the oldest church in the country, a cemetery with the tombs of chiefs and their families, and an historical rock that was used to crush skulls before putting the bodies into the pot.

Rakiraki

The building of Wananavu Beach Resort on the most northern point of Viti Levu, has brought a tourist boom to the Rakiraki area. The spot is about 2 hours drive from Nadi Airport, and about 3 hours from Suva, and boasts Fiji's highest sunshine hours. Rakiraki was the home of Ratu Udre (pronounced 'Ondre'), a 19th century chief and Fiji's last cannibal. His tomb is at the town junction and the 999 stones placed around it represent the number of people he ate.

The island of Nananu-i-Ra, just off shore, offers some of the best diving in the world.

Ten kilometres west of Rakiraki is **Navatu,** and a castellated rock that stands at 192m. It is famous in Fijian myth as one of the jumping-off places for new spirits. When Navatu was visited by Sir Arthur Gordon, in 1876, he found three villages on the rock, one at the foot, one half way, and the other on the summit. Apparently, when the villages were attacked, the women and children would take refuge at the top, while their men fought amongst the houses below.

Thirty-five minutes drive from Rakiraki is the mission church at **Navunibiti,** with its painting of the black Christ.

Travelling west from Rakiraki the next stop is **Tavua,** a large market town, and service centre for the Vatukoula Gold Mine.

Near here is the Yaqara Estate, a property of some 6900ha, which was established near the Nasivi River in 1926. It was operated by the Colonial Sugar Refinery as a cattle station, and it is not unusual to see cowboys as you drive through this district.

Ovalau

Situated off the eastern side of Viti Levu, this island is the home of the old capital, **Levuka.** It was the site of the Deed of Cession in 1874, and the waterfront looks much as it did a century ago. It is the centre of Fiji's fishing industry complete with canning factory. There is a road around the island linking villages with the airport at **Bureta** and the town of **Levuka.**

Westpac and National Bank of Fiji are represented in Levuka.

How to get there

Air Fiji, **ph 313 666,** flies twice daily to Bureta Airport from Nausori at 8am and 5pm and the fare is F$40 one way per person. The airline also offers a day trip in conjunction with Ovalau Tours and Transport (see Tours). Access is also by inter island ferry, and a car ferry operated by *Patterson Brothers,* **ph 315 644.**

Kadavu

A big island, 50km by 13km, Kadavu lies to the south of Viti Levu, and there is an airport at Vunisea.

At the northern end of the island is the famous Astrolabe Reef, well-known the world over. The biggest village on the island is

Vunisea, which sits on an isthmus, and other island attractions are the beautiful beaches at **Drue** and **Muani.**

Waikana Falls is close to the airport and is a great place for a swim, and west of the airport is the village of **Namuana.** This is where the local women can call giant turtles up from the sea by chanting to the ancestral spirits.

There are many interesting walks on the island, but it is always best to seek local knowledge about these, especially if you wish to walk to the summit of Nambukelevu, 838m above sea level.

How to get there

Sunflower Airlines, **ph 723 016,** flies there daily from Nadi at 1pm - one way fare F$76 per person.

Air Fiji, **ph 313 666,** flies to Kadavu from Suva on Mon, Wed and Fri at noon - one way fare F$59 per person.

Access is also available by inter-island ferry.

The Whippy ferry departs Millers Old Wharf in Suva on Tues and Fri at 6am, **ph 340 015.**

The Kadavu ferry departs Wed and Fri, **ph 311 766.**

Regarding finances, there are no banks on the island, so ensure that you have exchanged enough for your stay before leaving the mainland.

Vanua Levu

The country's second largest island is north of Viti Levu in the Koro Sea, a world famous diving site. Also, the soft corals of Somosomo Strait are thought to be amongst the most beautiful in the world.

Once the centre of the sandalwood trade, Vanua Levu's present economy depends on sugar and copra, and its main port is **Savusavu.** The principle urban centre is **Labasa** which is the third largest town in Fiji.

You can visit a copra plantation, a citrus orchard or take a full day tour to Labasa and surroundings. This is sugar cane country. There are plenty of cruises and all water sports are available.

Behind Morris Hedstrom is a hot spring that bubbles through the coral, and which the locals use to cook vegetables. Under no circumstances think of this as a place to bathe.

How to get there

Sunflower, **ph 723 408,** departs Nadi for Savusavu at 8am and 12.30pm, and the fare is F$110 per person, one way.

Air Fiji, **ph 313 666,** departs Suva for Savusavu at 8.15am and 2pm, and the fare is F$77 per person, one way; and departs Nadi at 7.45am on Mon, Wed, Thurs, Sat and Sun, and at 3pm on Mon, Tues, Thurs and Sat - F$110 per person, one way.

Sunflower departs Suva for Labasa at 8am and 4.30pm - F$82 per person, one way, and departs daily from Nadi at 7am, 9am and 3.30pm.

Air Fiji departs Suva for Labasa from Mon to Sat at 6.45am and 8.45am. and Sun at 8am and 10am. Daily flights depart at 2.45pm and 4.45pm - fare F$82 per person, one way; and from Nadi at 8am and 3pm.

The ANZ Bank, Westpac and National Bank of Fiji have branches in Savusavu and Labasa.

Taveuni

Known as the Garden island, Taveuni is the third largest island of the Fijian group, and was discovered by Abel Tasman in 1643. Torrential rainfalls on the south-east side, and to a lesser degree on the populated north-west side, along with rich volcanic soil and loads of sunshine, create this green paradise.

The 180 degree of longitude passes south of **Waiyevo,** in southern Taveuni, and in the early days the European planters could force their labourers to work seven days a week by having Sunday at one end of the property and Monday at the other. This devious practice came to an end in 1879 when a law was passed that decreed that all of Fiji was west of the dateline.

In the mid-1800s planters tried growing cotton on the island, but turned to sugar when the cotton market collapsed, and Taveuni was home to one of the country's first sugar mills.

In the interior of the island is **Lake Tagimocia,** a 900m high crater lake that has the rare *tagimocia* plant growing on its shores. The plant flowers once a year in mid-December, and efforts to transplant it to other areas have always failed. Legend says that a young woman was being forced by her father to marry a much older man, and was crying her little heart out beside the lake. As the tears touched the ground they turned to flowers, and when a bypasser reported this to her father he relented and allowed her to marry the man of her choice.

On the north-west coast is **Somosomo** and the chiefly village of **Cakaudrove,** which was the seat of Tui (King) Cakobau. One of Fiji's most important missionaries, William Cross, a victim of cannibalism, is buried in the village.

The east has many natural attractions, including the **Bouma Waterfall.** It cascades 20m into a deep pool that offers a chance for a refreshing dip.

Other places worth visiting are **Vuna,** the blow hole at **Namboundrau Bay,** and the **Waitavala Natural Waterslide.**

Today Taveuni is a mecca for divers and deep sea fishing freaks. The 31km Rainbow Reef is an amazing dive site where a huge range of sea life exists in only 5m of water.

One drawback to the island is the local transport. There is a bus service, but it is pretty infrequent, and taxis here are more expensive than anywhere else in Fiji.

How to get there

Sunflower, **ph 723 408,** flies to Taveuni from Nadi daily at 8am and 12.30pm - F$132 per person, one way.

Air Fiji, **ph 313 666,** flies to Taveuni from Suva daily at 2pm - F$98 per person, one way; and from Nadi at 7.45am on Mon, Wed, Thurs, Sat and Sun, and at 3pm on Mon, Tues, Thurs and Sat - F$132 per person, one way.

Access is also available by car ferry and inter-island shipping services.

There is a branch of Westpac Bank in Somosomo, and a branch of the National Bank of Fiji in Waiyevo.

Lau Group

This group of 29 islands forms the eastern section of Fiji. Hardly any tourists visit although there is some guest house accommodation, and the Lomaloma resort on the island of Vanuabalavu. There are airports on Lakeba, Vanuabalavu, Moala, Cicia and Ono-i-Lau. Yachts wishing to call at Lau must receive permission from the Secretary of Fijian Affairs, Suva.

Lakeba is the largest island in the group and has a population of around 2000, housed in eight villages. Its most important member is none other than Ratu Sir Kamisese Mara, the former prime minister.

Visitors to Lakeba could be forgiven for thinking that they had mistakenly landed in Tonga, for the Tongan influence is everywhere, in the houses, the clothing and the songs and dances. This is caused by the fact that the islands were overtaken and ruled by the Tongan warlord Ma'afu in the 1800s.

The village of **Nasaqalau** is home to the only Fijians who can call in the sharks, which they do every October and November. It seems that the village people can trace their origins to the village of Wainikeli on Taveuni, but they have brought their magic to this island and left none behind. Apparently this affinity with sharks also protects these people if their boats happen to capsize.

Nasaqalau also has many limestone caves, the largest being known as 'Pregnant Women's Cave' *(Oso Nabukele)*, because a woman who is trying to hide her pregnancy is not supposed to be able to slip through the cave's entrance. The Chief of the village will arrange a tour of the cave for F$5, but it is advised that you take your own torch (flashlight) so as to be able to see all the stalagmites and stalactites.

Qara Bulu is a smaller cave which was used as a gaol during tribal wars, and a third cave, *Koro-ni-Vono,* had a much more sinister use. If a person contracted tuberculosis he would be sealed in this cave, and the villages still say that you can hear the moans of the dying. If you wish to visit these two caves it is best to make enquiries in Nasaqalau.

How to get there

Air Fiji has scheduled flights from Nadi International Airport to Lakeba. Contact them on **313 666, fax 400 479,** for details of timetables and fares.

In the past it has been possible to obtain passage on a government vessel sailing to the Lau Group. To explore this avenue of travel contact the Visitors Bureau in Thomson Street, Suva, **ph 302 433, fax 300 970.**

Tours & Cruises

NADI

Nadi Town is great place to use as a tour base. There are many tours on offer, and following is a selection. It should be noted that many of these tours can also be taken from Coral Coast resorts and hotels, but the prices vary according to the distance travelled. The name of the tour company in each case is given, but the tours can usually also be arranged through your hotel.

Abaca National Park - full day tour - Mon, Wed and Fri - village visit, welcoming ceremony, sightseeing and hiking in Abaca National Park - pick up from Denarau hotels, Tanoa International, Tokatoka and Lautoka Park Boutique - Natural Tours Fiji, **ph 721 937.**

Adventure Fiji-Sabeto Trek - one day tour - daily - travel through cane fields to the highlands for views of the mountains and valleys overlooking the international airport - pick up from Denarau Island resorts and Nadi hotels - F$30 per person - Road Tours Fiji Ltd, **ph 722 935.**

Aqualand Cruise - full day and half day (morning or afternoon) - aboard 112ft Stardust II to Aqualand, an island water sports haven a half hour cruise from Denarau Marina - F$33 for cruise only, all water sports extra, bbq lunch F$11 - Nadi area hotel pick up - South Sea Cruises, **ph 722 988, fax 720 346.**

Bula Fiji Day Tour - full day guided tour of Suva, with stop at Orchid Island Fijian Cultural Centre - pick up from Nadi Hotels - F$56 - UTC, **ph 722 811, fax 720 107.**

Castaway Island Full Day Cruise - sail via Plantation Island on the schooner Seaspray which has full bar service and entertainment - Nadi area hotel pick up - F$59, resort activities extra - South Sea Cruises, **ph 700 144, fax 720 346.**

Coast & Country Tour - half day guided tour in 4WD touring coach, Garden of the Sleeping Giant, Indian temple, cane fields, Lautoka City and markets - Mon, Thurs and Sat from Nadi hotels only - departs 1.30pm, returns 5.30pm - F$39 adults, F$12 children, reservations essential - UTS, **ph 722 811, fax 720 107.**

Coral Coast Railway Co - evening train ride with cocktails and serenaders, disembark Sigatoka and Fijian warriors escort passengers to Nayawa Village for lovo dinner, kava ceremony, Fijian dances, village tour and craft demonstrations - return trip by coach - F$77 from Nadi hotels - Ben's Cultural Tours, **ph/fax 500 845.**

Fijian Cultural Day Tour - full day tour via the Queens Road - Fiji's past is recreated at the 'Island Village - tour the island in a native canoe - entertainment by the legendary firewalkers, or the Dance Theatre of Fiji - free time to spend at the Pacific Harbour Resort - pick up from Nadi hotels - F$54 - UTC, **ph 722 811, fax 720 107.**

Helicopter Tour - 20 minutes/45 minutes flight - take off from the Sheraton beach, fly over the Mamanuca Islands and the Nausori Highlands - narration - 20 minute flight F$107, 45 minute flight F$184 - Sheraton Tour Desk, **ph 750 385.**

Navala Village & Nausori Highland Safari - the village is located in the mountains of Ba - travel by air-conditioned 4WD to the Nausori Highlands via Lautoka City and Ba - lunch, morning and afternoon tea included - F$95 per person - Victory Inland Safaris, ph 700243.

Namuamua Inland Tour - scenic drive through the Coral Coast to the rice growing town of Navua - board open-water taxi for trip up the Navua River through the Namosi rainforests and waterfalls - kava ceremony and village tour - traditional lunch and Fijian dancing - F$79 per person, all inclusive - Optional Tours of Fiji, **ph 722 666.**

Pacific Harbour Cultural Centre and Marketplace Tour - depart Nadi Town at 8am for Pacific Harbour complex - Fijian dancing and singing (Mon, Wed, Thurs and Fri) - firewalking (Tues, Sat) - depart for Nadi Town at 4pm - price from Nadi Airport and Denarau Island hotels are the same F$71, lunch extra - Road Tours of Fiji, **ph 722 935.**

Plantation Island Day Cruise - leaves Denarau Marina at 9am aboard 27m schooner Seaspray for cruise to Plantation Island - lively crew entertainment and bar service - all water sports available for hire - resort facilities accessible to day trippers - free Nadi area hotel bus pick up - F$49 per person, includes lunch - South Sea Cruises, **ph 700 144, fax 720 346.**

Starlight Dinner Sail - an authentic tall ship sails from Denarau Marina to Vuda Point for an international dinner at 'First Landing Restaurant - return cruise includes Coffee and Bounty Rum Nightcap - departs 5.30pm, returns 9.30pm - f475 adult, F$37.50 child - Captain Cook Cruises, **ph 701 823.**

Sunday Blues Tour - visit local cane farms, the Gun Site at Morni Bay and stop at Seashell Cove Resort - enjoy all sporting facilities, a bbq lunch and cocktails - Optional Tours of Fiji, **ph 530 771.**

Surfing Day Trip - day trip from Seashell Cove to the Namoto Island breakers - F$25 per person - Seashell Cove, **ph 720 100.**

Suva Hibiscus Tour - air conditioned coach with tour escort - drive to Suva, lunch at Ming Palace, tour Orchid Island Cultural Centre - $59 for Nadi and Coral Coast areas - Optional Tours of Fiji, **ph 722 666, 722 608.**

Suva - City of Surprises Tour - depart Nadi at 8am - short stop at Pacific Harbour then on to Suva, past Government House and Albert Park - visit Fiji Museum - disembark at Suva Travelodge for $3^1/_2$ hours shopping and sightseeing - $46 Nadi/Denarau Island hotels - Road Tours of Fiji, **ph 722 935.**

3-D is Dynamic, Dramatic and Delightful - the three dimensions are Shotover Jet, Island Hoppers helicopters, and the Garden of the Sleeping Giant - two departures daily, 10am and 2pm - adults F$199, children (2-15 years) F$149, inclusive of VAT - Great Sights (Fiji), **ph 723 311, fax 720 184.**

Trek Mountain, Waterfalls & Fijian Village - hike in the mountains, visit waterfalls, swim in mountain creeks, all in the remote highlands - visit a bat cave, see a Fijian chief's bure, sample kava and experience the kava ceremony of welcome - F$47 per person, includes Fijian lunch and afternoon tea - Tourist Information Centre, **ph 700 243, fax 702 746.**

Whales Tale Champagne Sail Cruise - full day cruise aboard the magnificent 100' schooner *Whales Tale* - one day sail through the Mamanuca Islands - champagne, continental breakfast, special gourmet buffet lunch, all beverages free of charge - snorkel equipment free of charge, sunset cocktails and entertainment by the crew on deck - F$150 per person, VAT inclusive - Oceanic Schooner, **ph 722 455, fax 720 134.**

LAUTOKA

Blue Lagoon Cruises - daily departures to the island bays and cays of the Yasawa Islands - 2 day cruise minimum - Blue Lagoon Cruises, PO Box 130, Lautoka, **ph 664 336, fax 664 098** (more information in Accommodation section).

Beachcomber Day Cruise - sails 10am from Lautoka Wharf - 140' 3-masted schooner Tui Tai (or other vessel) - licensed bar and singing crew - fruit served aboard, Fijian lovo and buffet luncheon feast on island at 1pm - coral viewing and afternoon tea included - scuba, parasailing, skiing, semi-submersible trips, canoeing, windsurfing and snorkelling are extra charge - return to Lautoka by 5.15pm - Beachcomber Cruises, **ph 661 500.**

CORAL COAST

Most of the Nadi tours can include pick up at Coral Coast resorts and hotels. Check with your hotel tour desk.

Baravi River Cruise - daily departures at 10am and 2pm from The Fijian Resort - cruise the Sigatoka River to the village of Naroro - Fijian entertainment and a kava ceremony - Fijian Hotel tour desk, **ph 520 155.**

Coral Coast Railway - departs 10am each day for Natadola beach and a bbq - train returns at 4pm - reservations, **ph 520 599.**

Coral Coast Railway Co - evening tour with cocktails and serenaders - disembark at Sigatoka - Fijian warrior escort to Nayawa Village for a lovo dinner - kava ceremony, Fijian dances, demonstrations - tour ends at 8pm - F$66 from Coral Coast hotels - Ben's Cultural Tours, **ph/fax 500 845.**

Day Cruise - daily coach transfers to Nadi for South Sea Cruises trip to Mana, Castaway, Plantation or Combo and Aqualand Island Day Cruises - Mana D$85, Castaway F$80, Plantation and Combo F$75, Aqualand F$55 (lunch included) - South Sea Cruises, **ph 700 144, fax 720 346.**

Fijian Cultural River and Lovo Lunch Cruise - full day river tour - departs Sigatoka River jetty at 10am Tues, Thurs and Sat - village visit, kava ceremony, pottery making, mat weaving and Fijian dancing and song - bookings must be confirmed one day before tour - F$50 per person - Ben's Cultural Tours, **ph/fax 500 845.**

Fijian Unique Culture - Pottery Village Tour - half day tour to Nayawa Village - kava ceremony, entertainment, pottery making and activities - Mon-Fri 9am-1.30pm - F$25 per person - Ben's Cultural Tours, **ph 500 845.**

Magic Waterfall - full day guided tour, minimum 2 persons - departs 10.30am daily from Pacific Harbour International Hotel - explore Namosi interior, waterfall swimming, tropical rainforest - transfer on river taxi and raft down the Navua River on bilibili (bamboo rafts) - F$54 including VAT, including bbq lunch and soft drinks, **ph 450 180.**

Mountainbike Tours - guided half and full days tours for all levels of experience - include Lovo lunch - information slide show by appointment at 4pm at Tom's Restaurant, Korotogo, Sigatoka, Queens Road, **ph 520 697, fax 520 678.**

Navua River Village Tour - travel to Nukusere Village - refer Nadi Tours - F$78 Fijian Resort, F$76 Coral Coast Resort, F$61 Pacific Harbour - Road Tours of Fiji, **ph 722 935.**

Navua River Canoeing or Rafting Tour - full day - pick up from Coral Coast hotels from 9.30am - scenic tour and Navua River trip

- paddling instructions given by experienced boatmen to ensure participants safety - F$78 Coral Coast, F$66 Pacific Harbour - Road Tours of Fiji, **ph 722 935.**

Nayawa Village Evening Tour - departs 4.30 from Coral Coast hotels, returns approx 8pm - includes village tour, lovo dinner, war club dances, fan dances - held in chief's bure - Mon, Wed and Fri - F$52 per person.

Tavuni Historical Hillfort Cruise - departs Sigatoka River Jetty 9.30am, noon and 2pm every day except Saturday - visit the only Hill Fort on the Coral Coast - cannibal oven, house mounds 3300 years old, chiefs' burial ground, commoners' burial ground, killing stones - F$30 - Ben's Cultural Tours, **ph 500 845.**

SUVA

Bula Walking Tours - full day guided walking tour including the Fijian Museum, Parliament, Thurston Gardens, Historical Buildings and the Market - tours based at Fiji Museum - bookings ph 315 944 - more information from Mereoni Moce, **ph 315 177 fax 305 143.**

Levuka Day Trip - these fly out of Suva and Nadi, Mon-Sat - cost includes return airfares, ground transfers on Ovalau, full breakfast on arrival, guided town walking tour, lunch and two afternoon tours - information from Air Fiji, ph 313 666, or Ovalau Tours and Transport, **ph 440 611, fax 440 405.**

Orchid Island Fijian Culture Centre - 10 minutes drive from Suva on Queens Highway - guided tours - entertainment, **ph 361 128.**

Orchard Island Cultural Centre & Marketplace of Fiji/Firewalking - pickup from Suva Hotels at 9.30am - travel to Orchid Island, then on to Cultural Centre at Pacific Harbour, barbecue lunch, swim at beach - Tues & Sun see Beqa Firewalkers - other days visit the Dance Theatre of Fiji - Wilderness Ethnic Adventures Fiji, **ph 315 730, fax 300 584.**

Explore the Interior by Boat - full day tour by motorboat up Navua River past villages, farmlands, gorges, waterfalls and forests - Kava ceremony, village tour and Fijian lunch - departs Suva 9.30am - Wilderness Ethnic Adventure Fiji, **ph 315730 300584.**

Pacific Harbour Cultural Centre & Marketplace/Namosi Highlands Tour - full day guided tour on mini-bus - departs Suva hotels at 7am for Pacific Harbour - departs Cultural Centre at 9am for Namosi Village and old village site - snack lunch on riverside - arrive Suva 2.30pm - F$70 - Discover Fiji Tour, **ph 450 180.**

Rosie the Travel Service - offers all Suva full/half day tours - Suva and Pacific Harbour tours - daily transfers Suva/Pacific Harbour/Coral Coast/Nadi - 46 Gordon Street, Suva, **ph 314 436, fax 314 439.**

Southwick Garden Tour - 11 Milne Road, Suva - 90 minute tour of tropical gardens accompanied by well-known Fiji Horticulturist, Mrs Maureen Southwick - 7 minutes from Suva City - minimum of 5 visitors required for private tour - F$13.50 per person - includes home-cooked morning or afternoon tea, **ph 300 460.**

RAKIRAKI

Catholic Mission Tour - half day - departs Rakiraki Hotel at 8am, taxi or bus transport available - see the famous murals at Navunibitu Catholic Mission, portraying the Madonna and Black Christ - Rakiraki Hotel, **ph 694 101** (PO Box 31, Rakiraki).

Nananu-i-Ra Island Tour - full day tour - departs Rakiraki Hotel at 9.30am, returns at 4.30pm - lunch included, transportation provided - Rakiraki Hotel, **ph 694 101.**

Penang Sugar Mill Tour - half day - departs Rakiraki Hotel at 10am, returns at 2pm - taxi or hotel transport available - Rakiraki Hotel, **ph 694 101.**

OVALAU

Levuka Day Trip - full day Mon to Sat - includes return airfares, ground transfers on Ovalau, morning tea and lunch - see Fiji's first school, the first Masonic lodge in the South Pacific, the first social club, the first Roman Catholic, Anglican and Methodist churches in Fiji, and Nasova, the location of the signing of the deed of Cession to Great Britain in 1874 - extended trips are available and include breakfast, a tour to the Bishop's tomb, and a 'tea and talanoa' session in local home - Ovalau Tours and Transport, **ph 440 611, fax 440 405.**

SAVUSAVU

A Day on the Bay - day cruise from Savusavu 9.30am-4.30pm - sail to the lower part of the bay with a stop for swimming and snorkelling before lunch - sunset cruise departs between 3pm and 4pm, depending on season - returns about 6pm or 7pm - Emerald Yacht Charters, **ph 850 440, 850 344.**

Copra Plantation Tour - visit copra plantation and copra mill to see how oil is produced - Eco Divers, **ph 850 122, fax 850 344.**

Fijian Village Tour - includes 2-3 hours visit as an invited guest at a Fijian village - cost F$20 per person (min. 2) - Eco Divers, **ph 850 122, fax 850 344**.

Labasa Tour - full day tour to Labasa Sugar Mill - F$90 per person, including lunch (min. 2) - Eco Divers, **ph 850 122, fax 850 344.**

Rainforest/Waterfall Tour - half day walking tour through tropical rain forest to a series of mini waterfalls - see herbal remedy plants, swim - Fijian guides - F$25 per person - Eco Divers, **ph 850 122, fax 850 344.**

Water Sports

Diving

Aqua-Trek Nadi, along from Mama's Pizza on the Main Street, **ph 702 413, fax 702412,** can arrange dive travel in Fiji. Full range of dive gear available. Diver training courses start every week.

Scuba Bula (Fiji) Ltd, Seashell Surf & Dive, **ph 720 100, fax 720 294** (PO Box 9530, Nadi Airport). Has full range of PADI Certificate courses, beginners' dives and educational snorkelling trips. Spectacular wall, cave and shark dives.

Subsurface Fiji Limited, ph 666 738, fax 664 422. Sail on the Tui Tai, a three masted schooner (capacity 350 passengers), to Fiji's oldest and largest marine sanctuary surrounding Beachcomber Island for diving, water sports and feasting. PADI instructors and scuba training pool available. Courtesy bus to and from all Nadi and Lautoka hotels.

The Dive Shop, opposite the Post Office in Nadi, **ph 780 626.** PADI Openwater Course, which includes pool training, classroom and ocean dives, begins each Monday and Thursday. Daily dive

trips. Courtesy pick-up from hotels. Dive gear supplied free of charge on trips.

Tropical Divers Fiji, contact Sheraton Fiji Resort activities desk, or **ph 660 956** (PO Box 9063, Nadi Airport). PADI Certification courses and dive trips for beginners, intermediate and advanced. Free pool session any day.

Yacht Charter
Dau Wai I and II, South Sea Cruises, ph 750 445, fax 720 346. These are 7.5m water taxis that carry up to 20 people. Available daily for resort transfers, sightseeing, gamefishing and general charter.

Dulcinea, Musket Cove Resort, Malolo Lailai, ph 666 710 (PO Box 9176, Nadi Airport). A 17m Ketch, carries up to 22 people, available for day sails from Nadi, Lautoka or island resorts in the Mamanucas.

TV Seaspray, South Sea Cruises, ph 722 988, fax 720 346.
A 26m schooner (max 70 people) available for daily charter from Denarau Marina.

Topcat, South Sea Cruises, ph 700 144, fax 720346.
A 9.9m, 30 knot, fully equipped luxury catamaran. Air conditioned cabin, shower and toilet facilities, snack and bar service. 27 people maximum. Resort transfers, seafari sightseeing and general charter.

Water Taxis, South Sea Cruises, ph 750 4455, fax 720 346.
Ten boats, from 5.5m to 9.9m, with catamaran and mono hull designs of varying sizes and capacity, available daily for resort transfers, sightseeing, snorkelling trips, etc. @1ST PAR =

Whales Tale, 30.48m schooner with accommodation for 8 people, based at the Sheraton Royal Denarau Resort, **ph 722 455, fax 720 441** (PO Box 9625, Nadi Airport).

Game Fishing
Magic Cat, Bay Cruises Fiji, ph 722 676 (24 hours)
or Sheraton Operations Bure, **ph 750 777, ext 478.** 9m power cat with twin outboards. Completely rigged for deep sea fishing, island transfers, etc.

Topcat, South Sea Cruises, ph 700 144, fax 720 346.
9.9m luxury catamaran - see above.

Snorkelling/Handline Fishing Trips from Sheraton Fiji/Royal Denarau Resort or Denarau Island. Daily departure at 10.30am and 2.30pm. Snorkelling gear and fishing equipment provided. Contact Bay Cruises, **ph 722 696 AH,** or Sheraton Fiji Resort Beach Bure, **ph 701 777 ext 479.**

South Sea Cruises Sports Fishing, ph 710 445, fax 720 346, have boats operating out of the Denarau Marina and the Sheraton Royal Denarau Resort, Nadi Bay to the waters of the Mamanuca Group. Max 6 to 8 people per boat.

Sport Fishing on The Islander, Bay Cruises, Nadi, ph 722 696. 8.5m cruiser, fully equipped for sport or big game fishing. Sail anywhere in the Mamanuca Island Group from the Sheraton Fiji Resort. Island hopping day trips also available for up to 12 people.

LAUTOKA

Diving
Subsurface Fiji Limited, ph 666 738, fax 669 995.
Sail on the Tui Tai to Fiji's oldest and largest marine sanctuary surrounding Beachcomber Island for diving, water sports and feasting. PADI instructors and scuba training pool available. Courtesy bus to and from all Nadi and Lautoka hotels.

West Side Water Sports Ltd, ph/fax 661 462.
Fully serviced professional dive trips out of Lautoka to nearby islands and reefs. Beginners and experienced divers are catered for with certified PADI Rescue Diver, Divemaster and Dive Instructor on all dives. Daily departures at 9am from the Lautoka Wharf.

MAMANUCA ISLANDS

Diving
Aqua-trek, Mana Island, ph 702 413, fax 702 412.
Fiji's only PADI 5 Instructor Centre based on the island resort of Mana and in Nadi. Complete range of PADI courses and 4 dives a day as well as night diving. Day trip to Mana includes 2 dives and transfers to and from Nadi.

Beachcomber Island Resort and Subsurface Fiji Ltd, ph 664 422, fax 666 716, offers diving in the marine sanctuary off Beachcomber Island. Qualified divers must have proof of certification. For new divers there are PADI instructors and a dedicated SCUBA training pool. Free courtesy bus from Nadi and Lautoka hotels. Introductory dive F$85, 1 qualified dive F$65.

Castaway Diving, ph 661 233, fax 665 753.
Castaway Island is in the centre of the Mamanuca Group. Professional PADI instructors and dive masters, Free PADI Discover Scuba Program in the pool, and PADI open water certification. Also specialties such as deep diving, night diving and underwater photography.

Fiji Deep, ph 662 266 (on Tokoriki Island).
Special accommodation and dive packages available at Tokoriki and Matamanoa Island resorts. Night dives, Discover SCUBA courses, and shark feeding.

Inner Space Adventures, ph/fax 723 883.
Located on the Wailoaloa Beach, beside Horizon and Travellers Beach, Nadi. Daily dive trips at 9am for certified divers and beginners.

Musket Cove Divers, Musket Cove Resort on Malololailai Island, ph 722 488, fax 790 378. I
ntroductory Scuba Course ($1\frac{1}{2}$ hours, including a 40 minute dive) F$83; Second dive F$50. 5 day PADI certification course starts every Mon. $390 nightdiving and all courses through the Divemaster available. 2 daily boat dives for the certified diver. 1 tank F$55, 2 tank F$88. Packages available.

Yacht Charter
Beachcomber Cruises, ph 661 500, fax 664 496,
has many craft. Tui Tai, three master schooner, 350 passengers, day cruise, half and full day charters, overnight safari, sunset/cocktail cruise. Raikivi, motor sailer catamaran, 46 passengers, half and full day charter, lunch cruise, sunset/moonlight/cocktail cruise. Adi Wina, water taxi, 15 passengers.

Lea, Stardust Yacht Charters, Malololailai, ph/fax 668 628.
14m steel cutter with centre board, 3 double cabins plus crew quarters. Saloon, galley, bathroom/shower. Crew caters with Italian and local cuisine. Scuba equipment with compressor available.

Moorings Rainbow Yacht Charters, ph/fax 666 710
(PO Box 9024, Nadi Airport).
2, 3 and 4 cabin yachts available for bareboat charter with local guide or skipper. Based at Musket Cove Marina.

Ra Marama, Captain Cook Cruises, ph 701 823, fax 702 045.
Former Vice Regal yacht now available for day charter, 110' Brigantine, 72 passengers max.

Game Fishing
Castaway Gamefishing Club, ph 661 233, fax 665 753.
Sports and gamefishing facilities are available on the Castaway Cat. Morning, afternoon, full day and hourly charters are available. Located at Castaway Island.

Sportfishing, Mamanuca Water Taxi, ph 661 455 ext 309, fax 720 346. Charters available for fishing, snorkelling, sightseeing trips and island cruises. 6-8 people per boat.

YASAWA

Diving

Westside Water Sports, PO Box 7137, Lautoka, ph/fax 661 462.
Island Trader MV Tausala cruises to Yasawa Coral Gardens. Prince includes return transfers, all meals and accommodation, plus 3 complimentary dives - F$275 per person.

CORAL COAST

Diving

Dive with Sea Sports Ltd, ph 500 225 (PO Box 688, Sigatoka). Daily dive trips at 8am, 10am and 2pm from The Fijian Resort. PADI Training facility offers all Open Water and Advanced Certifications. Free pool sessions each day at 2pm.

Subsurface Fiji Limited, ph 666 738.
Spectacular dives in the marine sanctuary surrounding Beachcomber Island. Pick up from hotels and transfer to Lautoka by coach.

Warwick Dive Shop, ph 530 555, fax 530 010.
Daily dive trips. PADI and NAUI Advanced and Open Water Certification. Sites include Morgan's Wall, Warwick Fiji Reef, Naviti's Treasure and Golden Reefs.

PACIFIC HARBOUR

Diving

Beqa Divers Fiji, ph 361 088, fax 361 047 (PO Box 777, Suva). Diving in Beqa Lagoon. 12.8m Fiji Diver is designed for diving, and new Wreck dive on FV Tasu II. Daily diving/snorkelling trips and training courses from beginner to specialty. Professional instructors and dive guides.

Dive Connections (Fiji) Limited, ph 300 269, fax 450 539
(PO Box 14869, Suva). Daily dive trips leave 9am from Villa 16
River Drive, Pacific Harbour, for Beqa Lagoon. Fully equipped 40'
Scuba Queen. Rate for 2 tank dive/weights/lunch F$90, snorkelling
F$45.
Tropical Expeditions, **ph 450 380, fax 450 426.**
4 day dive cruises, day trips and charters available. Meals
provided.

SUVA

Diving
**Dive Centre (Fiji) Ltd. Located at Walu Bay, ph 300 599,
fax 302 639** (PO Box 3066, Lami). Trained maintenance
technicians. PADI Instructor certification courses, modern
workshop facilities and a complete range of retail dive equipment.

Nai'a Cruises/Live Aboard Scuba Diving, ph 450 382, fax 450 566
(PO Box 3179, Lami). 120' motor sailer, diving in Beqa, the
Lomaiviti Group, Namena and Lau (special charters). 8 double air
conditioned cabins, with private baths. Unlimited diving.

Ocean Pacific Club of Fiji, ph 304 864, fax 361 577 (PO Box
3229, Lami). Diving in Beqa Lagoon from 45' Bluewhale 2, large
dive deck, professional crew, hot showers. F$109 per person for 2-
tank dive. Available for 'live-aboard' and charter from one to five
nights.

Scuba Hire Ltd, 75 Marine Drive, Lami, ph 361 088, 361 047.
PADI 5-star training facility with private multi-level pool and
lecture room.

Tradewinds Divers, ph 361 088, fax 361 047.
Vessel Sundowner is located at Tradewinds Marina for dive trips to
main Suva reef. Night diving and snorkelling available.

Charter Yachts
Fiji Yacht Charter Association, ph 361 796.
Offers cruising for both the experienced and not so experienced yachts person.

Nai'a Cruises, ph 450 382, fax 450 566 (PO Box 3179, Lami).
102' luxury motor sailor with accommodation for 16 in 8 staterooms. Charters available from one day to up to three weeks.

Sere-ni-Wai, ph 361 171, fax 361 137 (PO Box 3256, Lami).
100' motor yacht, launched 1995, air conditioned cabins with private facilities. Contact Greg Lawlor.

Tau, ph 361 796, fax 361 035 (PO Box 3084, Lami).
27.43m steel ketch with accommodation for six. Private facilities. Based in Suva and the Lau Islands.

Game Fishing
Ocean Pacific Club of Fiji, ph 304 864, fax 361 577 (PO Box 3229, Lami). Live-aboard charter on the Adi Kuini at F$1100 per day. Includes accommodation, all fishing gear, all meals and professional crew. 8 hour charter, F$750, includes all tackle and lunch. Other vessels available.

RAKIRAKI

Diving
Ra Divers, ph 694 511, fax 694 899 (PO Box 417, Rakiraki). Located on Nananu-i-ra Island. A NAUI Pro Facility. Daily diving from two fully equipped dive boats. Dive packages and accommodation with meals arranged. NAUI and PADI dive instruction from open water to advanced.

OVALAU ISLAND

Diving
Ovalau Divers, ph 440 235 or 721 988.
Dive close to Levuka Town. PADI certificates, repair facility and snorkelling trips. Rates include 1, 2 and open water tank dives.

KADAVU ISLAND

Diving
Dive Kadavu Matana Resort, ph 311 780, fax 303 860.
Diving is less than 15 minutes from the Resort on the Namalata and Tavuki Reefs. The dive shop runs four dives daily, also night and shore dives. PADI courses, equipment rental, photo services available.

Galoa Island Divers, ph 315 703 (PO Box 6, Vunisea, Kadavu). Located at Reece's Place. Introductory lesson is free, single dives F$30, double dives F$50, shore dive F$15, including tanks and weights. Other courses start from F$260, including gear.

Malawai, ph 520 102, fax 305 060 (Malawai), 361 159, fax 361 536 (Suva). (PO Box 1277, Suva).
Diving at Malawai's off-shore reefs and the only wreck (210', 675 tons) in Kadavu. Features hard and soft corals, swim throughs, overhangs and abundant fish life. PADI instructor, top dive gear and aluminium boats including the Adi Lee, 32', twin Cummins powered.

Matava, ph 336 098, fax 336 099 (PO Box 63 Kadavu).
Located near the Great Astrolabe Reef. Diving, with two PADI instructors, include boat, tank and weights from F$35. Multi-dive packages available from F$200. Instruction for Open Water, advanced, rescue, Dive Master.

Naiqoro Divers, ph 302 896.

Based at Albert's Place, this is a small diving operation that caters for groups of up to six divers without gear and nine divers with gear. Rates include single boat dive F$35, double boat dive F$65, shore dives F$20. For night dives add F$10.

Nukubalavu Adventure Resort and Dive Centre, ph 520 089 (island), 314 554 (Suva), fax 302 212 (PO Box 686, Suva).

Based on eastern Kadavu, near the Great Astrolabe Reef. Discover scuba course F$75, dives from F$40, daily equipment rental F$15. PADI instruction for open water certification (4-6 days) F$295. Advanced certification, rescue diver certification, diver master certification also available.

Game Fishing

Malawai, ph 520 102, fax 305 060, Suva ph 361 159, fax 361 536 (PO Box 1277, Suva). Fish aboard the 32' twin Cummins powered, fully-equipped Miss Conduct. Charter rates include full day at US$500, half day US$350. Light tackle trolling off the Malawai reefs on Taki Mai.

SAVUSAVU

Diving

Eco Divers, ph 850 122, fax 850 344 (PO Box 264 Savusavu). Embark at the Copra Shed Marina complex in Savusavu town. Dive Masters operate two large twin engined Zodiacs fitted out for multiple dives. 10 tank dive package. Dusk dives and night dives are also available. They have an initial offer of 2 tank boat dive F$85 per person.

Kontiki Resort, ph 850 352 and ask for Dive Shop. PADI Dive facility with trips to Savusavu Dream House. Full instructional services on site from beginner to Assistant Instructor. Accommodation packages with the resort.

L'Aventure Cousteau/Cousteau Fiji Islands Resort, ph 850 188, fax 850 340.

A full service shop offering equipment and guided trips to the best sites in the area. Instruction and PADI certification offered for underwater naturalist, photographer and more. On-site photo processing and tips from marine scientists are also available.

Namale Resort, ph 850 435, fax 850 400.

Fully equipped dive shop with fast dive boats, and PADI dive masters and instructors.

Game Fishing

Sportfishing, ph 850 122, fax 850 344 (Eco Divers, PO Box 264, Savusavu). 32′ powercat Kontiki One. Cost F$100 per hour, F$400 half day, F$750 full day.

TAVEUNI

Diving

Dive Taveuni Resort, ph 880 441, fax 880 466 (Dive Taveuni, Matei PO, Taveuni Island). Diving is available from Fiji's largest (40′) catamaran, which is custom-designed for diving. 2 tank dive US$82. Hire gear available.

Rainbow Reef Divers/Garden Island Resort, ph 880 286, fax 880288 (PO Box 1, Waiyevo, Taveuni). Daily excursions on offer to world-class dive sites. For the novice there are PADI discover scuba, learn-to-dive and advanced courses.

Noks Dive, ph 880 246 (PO Box 22, Taveuni).
Located at the waterfront off Kris Pack Palace, this facility provides a variety of dive experiences.

Lady Christine, ph 880 260, fax 880 274 (Matagi Island Resort, PO Box 83, Waiyevo, Taveuni). 42' cabin cruiser and a 43' outboard powered vessel. Dive packages include two boat dives a day, weights, tanks and unlimited shore diving. Full certification courses and resort courses are also offered.

Susie's Plantation Dive Centre, ph/fax 880 125 (PO Box 69, Waiyevo, Taveuni). World class dive sites. 2 tank dives from F$77, dive package F$363. Full dive courses and dive packages on request. Full range of Sherwood rental equipment.

Dive Laucala Fiji Forbes, ph 880 077, fax 880 099.
World class diving. All equipment supplied, no schedules (dive as often as you like). Full service photo-video lab on premises, video and still camera hire, E6 processing, custom video, available for purchase. Full PADI certifications and resort courses also available.

Yacht Charter
Seax of Legra, ph/fax 880 141 (PO Box 89, Waiyevo, Taveuni), a 14m sailing ketch based at Taveuni. Maximum 4 people in two cabins, two shower/toilet compartments. Fully crewed with skipper and gourmet chef. Day and extended cruises off north-eastern islands including Northern Lau Group.

MV Matagi Princes II, ph 880 260, fax 880 274
An 85' luxury vessel with 6 air conditioned cabins, each with own facilities. 4, 5 and 6 nights scheduled departures. Extended charters are available.

INDEX

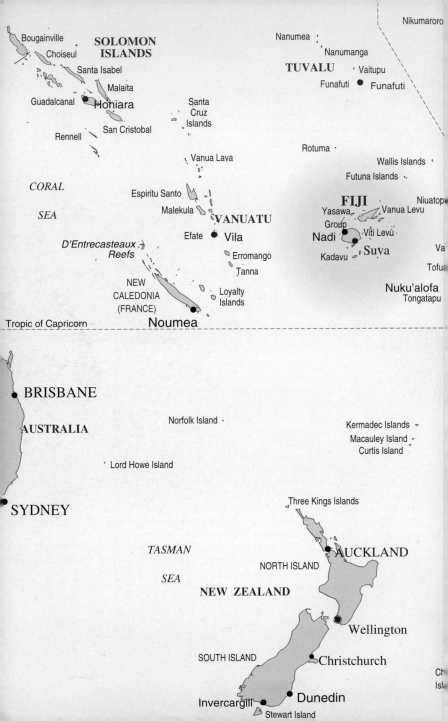